SECOND CHANC

SECOND CHANCE RUNAWAY

SECOND CHANCE RUNAWAY

SECOND CHANCE RUNAWAY

SECOND CHANCE RUNAWAY

Donna Buchanan

EDITOR

Lucinda F. Boyd

SECOND CHANCE RUNAWAY

Copyright

ACKNOWLEDGEMENTS

Thank you to everyone!

I want to thank God for guiding me in life and showing me my dream.

Mom, I want to thank my Mom for her prayers and always believing in me and encouraging me to always follow my dream. I'm sorry for all the hurt I caused you throughout the years. You never counted me out and for that I will always be grateful. You taught me to always follow my heart and encouraged me to reach out to the youth today and share my story so that I might help others. I will be forever indebted to you! You are my biggest inspiration.

George Reres, my lawyer I want to give you thanks, you saw something in me that first day you met me. You saved my life and you were the first person to reach out to me. You saw beyond my past and saw a future for me. Throughout the years you would continue to encourage me to better my life. I want to thank Dr. Lenore Walker, Dr. David Shapiro, Dr. Sherri Bourg-Carter, Dr. Meryl Rome, Suzanne and my whole legal team for believing in me at the very beginning. You were my dream team and without your belief in me I might not have been given a second chance.

I want to thank Rob and Lucinda Boyd my managers for reaching out to me in prison July 4, 2012 a year before my release after seeing my story on Wetv. You told me about your movement, The Streets Don't Love You Back. Here was a way for me to tell my story and help people not go down the same road I did. Thank you both for believing in me. You were both there for me my very first day out and encouraged me to write my autobiography and live out my dream. You both have been such an inspiration to me as well as countless others. Both of you believed in me and helped me share my story.

To my manager and editor, Lucinda Boyd, Thank you very much for believing in my story and the countless hours you spent typing and editing my book. May God bless you always.

I want to thank Beverly and Ferd Sebastian with the National Greyhound Foundation and Second Chance at Life Prisoner Partner-ship program. You have helped countless women with your program and have given so many second chances at life. The work you do with the retired greyhound dogs is truly remarkable and your belief in helping others. Your passion has become my passion and I will always be grateful to the both of you. You also believed in me and what I am doing.

I would like to thank the staff at Gadsden Correctional Institution Captain Crutcher, Ms. Jackson, Mr. Rogers, Mr. Giannini, Mr. Brown, and Mr. Moore. To all the girls still inside Virginia, Donna,

SECOND CHANCE RUNAWAY

Kelly, GiGI, Dixie, Ashley, Heather, Michelle, Perez, CeeCee, Cassy, Judith, Carolyn, Angela, Angelina and Kristy you are not forgotten. I believe in all of you and I'm so proud of all the accomplishments each and every one of you has achieved. To Virginia, My little baby you made me laugh and you brightened up even the hardest days in prison. I will always be your "Grammy". I'm so proud of you and I can't wait till you come home. To GiGi, You have come so far in your journey. You are truly a remarkable woman and I'm proud to call you my friend. You have a wonderful future ahead of you and I believe in you. May God always bless you in life. I would also like to thank the staff at the Suncoast work release center, Ms. Cullen, Ms. Sherman, Ms. Dunmoore, and Ms. Saydeh for always listening to me when I just needed to talk. You helped my transition back into society and your passion for your girls is beyond praise. You believed in each and every one of us.

Partial proceeds from the sales of my book and on-line store will go to The Streets Don't Love You Back Movement and The National Greyhound Foundation.

WEBSITES

www.facebook.com/SecondChanceRunaway

www.lulu.com/spotlight/secondchancerunaway

SECOND CHANCE RUNAWAY

A SECOND CHANCE AT LIFE

As I walked into the filled courtroom, I asked myself how did I end up facing a 2nd degree murder charge? The courtroom was full that day and I remember how nervous I felt even though I already knew what was going to happen. But what stays in my mind is the surprise I felt when I looked around. I thought I would be facing this day by myself but what I saw was the faces of people who cared about me and my future. My whole legal team was there and they believed in me. I think that was a revelation for me at that moment in my life. The first time there was any awareness that I was not just a drug addict but a person and this didn't have to be the end. My lawyer George Reres was there along with Dr. Lenore Walker, Suzanne Mignone, Dr. Shapiro, Dr. Sherri Bourg- Carter and the rest of my legal team. They were all smiling at me and offering me strength. I felt my knees about ready to give out as the deputy escorted me to my seat. George smiled at me and squeezed my hand giving me strength as I faced the judge. I took a deep breath resigned to my future and looked over at George. I trusted him and I knew he only had my best interest at heart. He wasn't just a lawyer to me, he had become someone I could depend on and who understood my life. He never judged me but genuinely cared, how rare that was for me. Here I was putting my life in someone else's hands and I knew I could do that with him. I knew he would not use me or harm me in any way. He had fought so long and hard for me showing the state I deserved to be spared. He was fighting, to finally give me the opportunity to have some kind of a life in the future. He wanted to help me rehabilitate my life not just get me a better sentence but a second chance at life. As I stood up to face my charges the noise in the courtroom faded away and I felt detached as the judge read the charge of 2nd degree murder. I couldn't hear what the judge was saying because the blood was pounding in my head and my life was flashing before my eyes. I was asking myself how did I get to this point in my life, how did it get so out of control. But the answer was simple but yet not so simple......

SECOND CHANCE RUNAWAY

I grew up in a middle class home. We lived in Portsmouth, Virginia in a suburb called Sweetbriar. I have nothing but happy memories of that place. When I was 7 we moved to a farm in Cumberland, Va. It was different going from city living to country living but I loved animals so I was able to surround myself with dogs and horses. They soon became my friends and I would roam around the farm with them. I always loved the outdoors and I was hardly indoors. I used to sit out in the snow with my German shepherds or hike through the woods. I was a normal kid but very shy as most young girls are at that age. We were very active with the church and I used to go to a Christian retreat in the summer time. We also used to go camping in the mountains for a couple weeks every summer. My parents used to argue a lot and I saw they weren't happy together. I knew my mom stayed with my father because of the kids. They treated us good. I remember Christmas time was always a very special time of year. My moms' father was in the navy so they moved around a lot and that's why she tried to make a staple environment for her kids. It was lonely living in the country and I was by myself a lot. My parents had bought a grocery store in town and my father had not only the farm to take care of but a construction company as well. So I was alone most of the time. We looked like the perfect middle class family. But in reality it wasn't so picture perfect, but I've found out a lot of families aren't always what they seem to be on the outside. I learned at an early age not to show people what was going on and to act like everything was okay.

I became skilled at hiding things at an early age. Till this day I have to catch myself when I go to say everything is okay when it's not. You cannot leave things bottled up inside of you because it will come out eventually. I've learned now to work through my emotions and to share them. By the time I was 12 years old boys and men started to show an interest in me. I was always attracted to older guys' maybe because they were the first to show me any attention.

My first boyfriend was 18 years old and I was 13 years old. I used to meet him at ballgames and school. He would call me on the phone which would later get me in trouble with my parents and make them aware that I was getting involved with young men.

One day a girl called me on the phone and asked why I was seeing her boyfriend. I soon discovered he was seeing both of us and I remember how much it hurt me. Instead of us getting mad at each other which most teenage girls do we both planned to meet him at a football game the following week and both of us approached him at the same time. We broke up with him right then and there and became best friends. Her name was Nancy and we would become inseparable throughout the years till this day. We started hanging out smoking and drinking and occasionally experimenting with light drugs mainly smoking pot.

One day I was down at the river swimming when a group of guys came up and started talking to me. There was one man that really stood out and we started talking and hung out the rest of the day together. He was 26 years old and I was only 14 years old at the time. After that day I used to ride my horse to meet him down at the river or somewhere near my house. We used to go swimming or just hang out on the banks of the river. I was very attracted to him and it made me feel special that someone so much older than me was that interested in me. One day he asked me to meet him so that night I climbed out of my bedroom window and walked down the road to a little church to where he was parked waiting for me. I was nervous and excited at the same time because this was the first time I had done anything like this. He had his brother and his girlfriend with him so we weren't alone which made me feel more comfortable. We went driving and he bought some beer. I soon became intoxicated and all worries about being out without my parents' approval went right out the window. I was young and I thought I was in love, here was a man much older, showing me all this attention and I was eating it up. It ended up getting real late, in fact too late to sneak back in my bedroom window. So instead of going back we took off together. We drove to the next county where he lived but we didn't go to his house because he was married and instead we went to some empty house that he knew wasn't occupied at the time. His brother stayed with us the whole time.

My parents soon discovered I was missing and contacted the police. His parents told him to turn himself in that the situation was getting out of control. We both rode back in the police car together. I remember I didn't want to go back and I was even upset with Jerry because I wanted to stay with him. I didn't want to deal with my father. Our relationship wasn't good and I just felt uncomfortable at home. It no longer felt right to me. It was getting to the point at home where I would stay in my bedroom all the time and I wouldn't come to dinner anymore unless my father made a big deal out of it so I didn't want to go back to that. I also knew Jerry was in trouble and I had no idea what my father would do. So I held his hand as we rode back to the Cumberland County Jail. Jerry went to jail and I went home to face my parents.

Nowadays he would have been labeled a pedophile but back then he was just charged with statutory rape and soon released from the county jail. I was court ordered to go to counseling and was angry at my father for forbidding me to see him ever again. I think that's when the resentment to my father began to get worse and our relationship really began to deteriorate. I mean things were already bad between us but this just made our relationship strained and awkward. He was always very judgmental of not only me but everyone else as well. I now see he was just concerned for my welfare but back then he was hurting the man I loved. My father and I have always had some kind of conflict.

After a little while I no longer had to go to counseling but I was still troubled and nothing had changed with family life. I started smoking pot more often and discovered pills made the pain go away. My parents took me to the town Doctor and he was prescribing narcotics for me because they saw me as a troubled child and their answer was to medicate me. I was still upset over Jerry and I was having a lot of problems with my dad and the shame I felt over Jerry.

Everyone believed I was ruined and no longer had a virgin because I had run away with him. In a small town everyone gossips and what was worse was my father believed it along with everybody else. My own family was judging me. I wasn't ruined but nobody believed me. I was still a virgin. I was at school telling Nancy I couldn't take it anymore and that I was going to run away. She talked me out of it telling me how much it would hurt my mom. My mother was my soft spot so as soon as she put my mom in it I knew I couldn't run away. So I told her I was going home and I would talk to her later.

As I was leaving school my brother in law was driving by and offered me a ride. I got in his pickup and I remember I was crying. I told him I was on my way home and I started to look out the window with tears flowing down my face. After a little while I noticed we weren't heading to my house. I asked him where he was going and he said he had to make a detour. He drove me out into a secluded part of the woods and parked his truck. I asked him what we were doing there. I was very confused and already so upset. Everything happened so fast after that. He got out of the truck and came over to my side of the truck opening the door and started to rape me. I remember fighting back, screaming at him and asking him why he was doing this. He ignored me and then I felt frozen, detached from what was happening and I tried to put myself somewhere else where there wasn't so much pain. No girl should ever lose their innocence through an act of violence.

Afterwards I felt I was ruined for any man and I blamed myself thinking I could have somehow stopped this from happening. How could I tell my father I was raped and would he even believe me. He already thought I was ruined and now I believed he would think this was my entire fault and blame it all on me. Our relationship was already bad so how could he believe me. These were all the thoughts that were going through my head. I had no one to turn to but that decision wasn't left up to me. He got in the driver's seat and started to drive towards Richmond. I sat in the cab of the pickup silently crying not saying a word as my whole world fell apart. I was very scared and I didn't know where he was taking me or what he was going to do next. He drove 60 miles to Richmond and then pulled over on the side of the road. I knew he was leaving me there and I just wanted to get away from him. He just turned around and looked at me as I got out of the truck. As the truck pulled away I had a feeling of complete despair. I had no one to turn to and this would soon become a pattern for me. Whenever a situation became unbearable for me instead of dealing with it I chose flight instead of fight.

I found myself alone in a city with nowhere to go. It wasn't long before someone stopped and asked me if I needed a ride. I was still crying and he was asking me what was wrong and telling me he could help me. I looked around and with a feeling of defeat got into his car. I was in the worse possible neighborhood and didn't know what to do. I could either stay out in the street or take my chance going with someone. I got in the car and rode off with the man. This would be a big mistake and I've tried to block this part out but I know I need to share it. If it helps one person than the pain it causes me to write about it is worthwhile. I'm not going to hide my past or my feelings anymore. I've done that all my life and I'm not ashamed of my past. It's a testimonial and I'm going to share it and educate others.

I was taken to a house where I was gang raped. There were about three or four young men there and I can't remember how long it went on. Until finally someone had the mind to say they needed to get rid of me because of my age. I was totally traumatized by that point. I found myself back out in the streets and once again lost and scared. I wondered around for a long time just walking going nowhere in particular because I had nowhere to go. I was tired, hungry and lost and just wanted to get off the streets. I was standing in front of a store when a car pulled up and a man was asking me if he could help me. The man was in his 30's and I didn't even hear what he was saying to me. I was trying to just block everything out trying to put myself somewhere else. I ended up getting in his car hoping that I could trust him and he would help me. He was just another predator preying on a young girl. He took me to his house where he had sex with me. I was only 14 years old a child scared and afraid. I was taking pills trying to block the pain but it wasn't working. I was terrified of this man and I wanted out of this situation. Then another man came and I began to get really frightened. My instincts told me things were about ready to go to a whole other level. So I snuck out of the house and hid in the bushes while they looked for me. Thankfully it was dark outside and they couldn't see me hiding. This situation was about to get bad. I might have been young but I knew they were going to hurt me. I stayed hidden and then I ran down the street to a gas station. There was a trucker there who offered to give me a ride. He saw I was frightened and then the two men started to come near the gas station. That's all it took, I was more afraid of the two men then I was of this trucker. So I told him these two men were after me and he told me to get in his truck and hide in the sleeper. The two men were asking the guy who worked at the gas station if he had seen a young girl. They came up to the truck I was hiding in and I heard them yelling with the trucker. I think they figured I was inside but they were drawing attention to themselves. I stayed hidden in his sleeper until they gave up. I learned at a very young age that there are all kinds of predators out there for young girls. The trucker was just another one out of many out there maybe in a nicer form but still a predator.

It's strange but I wouldn't think of it in that way until I was in prison maybe because I had time to reflect on my life and face the darkness that I hid inside of myself and the more I educated myself and worked with the young girls in prison it all became very clear to me. I want to stress that there is help out there for runaways. Call a hotline seek help don't put yourself in a situation that you might not make it out of. I know God was protecting me. There are men out there killing women everyday especially runaways. A lot of young girls are never found.

The Trucker drove off and we started driving out of the state. He said he was headed for Texas and at that point I just didn't care anymore. Too much was happening and I was still too traumatized to say anything. After a few days with him I knew I had to get away. I couldn't stand it when he touched me and I knew it wasn't right. When we stopped at a hotel one night there were a bunch of marines in the room next to us having a party, I went over there and started to hang out and one of them was heading back to his base. I asked him if he would give me a ride and he said he could take me for a little ways. I left with him and he let me out a few hours later. I started hitchhiking and ended up in Texas. I was just catching rides never staying in one place. Then I started heading back towards Virginia. I didn't have any particular direction in mind I was just running. I ended up in Portsmouth, Virginia close to where I had grown up in Sweetbriar. I think that place represented all that was pure and innocent in my life. Till this day I still think about that place with longing. I remember I was at a gas station talking to the attendant. He was a young man and was very nice to me and he let me call my friend's mother to come get me. While I was outside waiting for my ride a man walked into the gas station and I heard a lot of yelling and soon the man ran outside. He had blood all over his hands and then I heard sirens. My friend's mother arrived at that moment and told me to get in the car. Later on I heard on TV that the young man had been stabbed over a botched robbery.

My friends' mother called my family and Mom and Dad sent my brother to bring me back home. Life back home was worse than ever and I knew I couldn't stay there. My sister didn't believe that Tommy had raped me and that made it worse. It made me feel bad and I continued to blame myself for what had happened. I don't think she really believes that it happened to this day. I was just a liar who made it up and the way I feel now is if I'm willing to say I was a drug dealer, a user, a prostitute, and a murderer... what am saying or thinking... I was raped!

It kind of ranks a little low on the totem pole, don't you think? It is what it is.

SECOND CHANCE RUNAWAY

One day my friends' mother called me telling me that Nancy had run away and asked me if I knew where she was. I knew exactly where she was so my Mother allowed me to go with her mother to Charlottesville to try and find her. There was a place called the Corner where everyone hung out especially runaways. I told Nancy's mother she would have to leave me alone or otherwise no one would talk to me. She reluctantly left and it wasn't long before I knew where Nancy was. I made a contact and had someone drive me there and once again best friends were back together. I started getting high with Nancy, smoking pot and decided I had nothing to go back to. Here was my opportunity to leave home and I decided not to go back to meet Nancy's mom. One thing that I regret most about that time was leaving her mother waiting there for me to come back and then having to call my mom and tell her she had lost me too. That still bothers me to this day and I never had a chance to tell Nancy's mother that I was sorry for leaving her there waiting for me not knowing if something bad had happened to me. Nancy ended up going back but I stayed out in the streets.

I become involved with my first drug dealer who was in his 30's. I remember he had a cabin up in the mountains right outside of the Charlottesville city limits. I would go into his house and it was nothing to see big bowls of cocaine lying around. I remember he had a birthday party and instead of gifts he got drugs for presents. I received a bale of marijuana, a key of coke or a huge crystal bowl of mescaline. I would leave him for short periods of times and roam the streets of

Charlottesville and then I would return. He never questioned me when I would leave or even when I came back. It was dangerous out on the streets and there were times I would run into some bad situations. I was raped again during that time on the streets in Charlottesville. It wasn't always happy times getting high and being on my own. It was a game of survival and I would see some of the runaways beaten up or some would disappear and we wouldn't know if they went back home or if something bad happened to them. I would often meet my mother in Charlottesville and she told me my sister was moving to Ft. Lauderdale with her husband and that I could go stay with her. I was ready for a break and wanted to get off the streets so I flew down there. My father drove me to the airport and that turned out to be a big mistake. He called me a whore and all kinds of names. He put me on the plane with no money and turned around and left. I vowed then that I would never again have anything to do with him. As far as I was concerned my father was dead. I still don't speak to him to this day though I have put the past behind me and have forgiven him. My heart is at ease and God has given me peace inside.

I had a layover in Atlanta, Georgia and I called my Mom all upset. I wasn't even 16 years old yet and the only one that held me together was my Mom. She was my lifeline and I didn't realize I was heading towards a disaster at my sister's house. Living with the man that had raped me did not go over well for me. I felt very uncomfortable in that situation so I would take off a lot. The bad thing was he continued to make sexual advances at me and at the same time was telling me how sorry he was. He ended up finding some drug paraphernalia and taking it to my sister telling her he didn't want me living there. She was pregnant with her first child and said she couldn't handle it so she kicked me out in the streets. I was barely 16 years old and once again back out with their nowhere to go and no one to turn to. There was an older man that lived next door and my sister encouraged me to live with him. He seemed like a very nice man until I found out how nice he wanted to be. As soon as he tried to molest me I was gone.

I was getting used to roaming the streets and I felt more at ease out there I was getting stronger and tougher and the streets had begun to educate me. I became involved with the Outlaws and they were actually very protective over me. I wasn't afraid of them; they were like my big brothers. They used to watch over me and I knew as long as I was with them no harm would come to me in that neighborhood. I met this Vietnam vet through them and he loved to make silencers in his place. This dude was still in the war and loved all kinds of weapons. He also used to sell drugs and he used his own product too. I remember one night he was showing a potential customer some napalm he had for sell. The guy wanted him to show him an example and the next thing I know the apartment building was on fire and you can't put napalm out that easy so the police showed up and I took off. After things settled down I was back hanging around with him. I felt safe with him and he never made me feel uncomfortable and just let me be, giving me space.

I ended up meeting a guy in the neighborhood and we started living together. We started selling drugs and got an apartment together. Let me tell you dating a detective's son can have its benefits especially when you're selling drugs. None of the cops would mess with us and it gave us a sense of security. I was getting more out of control with my drug use, no longer just selling but using heavily. This went on for a few years. I started using heavier drugs but hadn't yet started using opiates, mainly cocaine, quaaludes, acid and hash. The block I lived on, 40th street was known for selling drugs. You had a house for cocaine, one for pot and another for heroin and so on. I sold quaaludes and coke mainly. My dealer lived across the street so it was easy for me to keep my supply going. Or I could go to the vet and pick up deals and make money. One night a dude that lived in the efficiency next to me come over and said he had a buyer for an ounce of coke. Now we always watched the neighborhood and we knew when there was a car that didn't belong. I had been scoping out the neighborhood and man there were cars all over that didn't belong. Being on the streets as I had been you learned to follow your instincts and my instincts were telling me straight up, this was a setup. I told this dude we had to take a ride so my boyfriend and I took off and as we drove down the road I knew we had to play this right or we were going down. We drove around for a while and then turned down 40th street. As soon as we took the turn cop cars and undercover cars blocked both ends of the street. I was actually pretty amazed at how many cars there were. I mean the whole street was lit up with lights so we drove really slowly. They let us reach our place and then we were pulled out of the truck with guns pointed at our heads. They were yelling at us and I remember one detective telling my boyfriend that his dad wasn't going to get us out of this one. Well I knew we were straight as long as we kept our cool because they had nothing on us unless they had a search warrant for our house. If they had a warrant for the house we were going down for real. They had nothing on tape and we had no product on us so therefore, no probable cause. They searched our truck and after finding nothing got the dogs out and started searching the block thinking we had thrown it out the window when we hit the block. After about an hour of searching they finally gave up and had to release us. Sure enough they didn't have a search warrant for the house.

I remember thinking man this was too close and I could have ended up in prison for a long time. We were so shaken up we didn't even go in the house for hours. We then watched our neighbors search the street themselves looking for the drugs everyone thought we had tossed. I was thinking man this is crazy, look at these crazy fools. We finally went inside loaded up some drugs and took off to Naples for a week to chill. We found out later from his Dad that they were after our neighbor and didn't even suspect us. He knew nothing about the bust. Our neighbor wasn't as lucky, they busted him for possession and conspiracy. We came back from Naples and resumed business as usual, once again confident of the game. My brother moved down to Ft. Lauderdale and stayed with me for a short time until he found an apartment across the street from me. We had always been very close growing up even though he was six years older than me. We used to drink a lot, smoke pot and travel up to Virginia together. Throughout the years I would remain close with him until later on then we would become estranged. My relationship began to deteriorate with my boyfriend and I started taking off a lot. I came home one night and told him I was moving out. He had become very controlling and jealous. He no longer wanted to work and I felt all the responsibility of supporting the both of us. He started tripping on me and pulled a shotgun, pointed it at me and pulled the trigger. I remember thinking I'm dead... I am so dead. I didn't even realize I was screaming. His Dad heard the blast from one block over and came running over to our house. I was still standing and I couldn't understand why I was still standing but I was afraid to look down afraid of what I would see. By then his dad was asking me if I was okay and I kept saying I'm shot because there was no way he could have missed me not at point blank range. He kept telling me I was fine and I looked down and sure enough there was no gunshot wound. What had happened was the shells were blanks so all I had was some minor burn marks from the gunpowder. He just wanted to scare me. He was trying to frighten me into staying with him. I knew after that that I had to get out of there or things weren't going to end right. It did hurt me leaving him and I knew it was hurting him as well but I couldn't handle the situation. His dad told me to leave that he would handle his son. So I took off and went to stay with my girlfriend Judy. I would remain very close with her until I later went to prison, her letters coming less frequently until they stopped coming at all.

I started shooting up cocaine by then and was using more than I was selling until I finally went out of business. I knew this guy who lived on the Ft. Lauderdale strip at the Mark 2100 club. He said I could stay there and clean out. He had catamarans and rented it out to tourists and had a little tiki hut that he sold suntan lotion out of. I was enjoying life on the beach and quit using the harder drugs just drinking and smoking pot. I used to go sailing during the days and clubbing at night. Life was good and it was very peaceful living on the beach. There was no hassle from him and we worked well together. I did my thing and he did his thing.

One night I came home and there were these three guys there. I asked my friend what was up and he pulled me aside and explained that one of the dudes wanted us to let his friend stay here for a little while because the guy was a pilot and he had dropped a load of drugs in the ocean on the way back from Columbia because he thought he was about to get popped and now the people who had paid for it was after him. I was okay with it; this craziness was becoming the norm in my life so we started drinking. The guy who was in charge started coming on to me real strong. I was quite taken with him and was instantly attracted to him. My friend had already told me he was married so I told him I wasn't willing to get involved as long as he was married. He told me the relationship with his wife was over and he was getting a divorce. I really didn't believe him but I continued to hang out with him the whole evening. He took me to a night club called Yesterdays and we drank and had a good time. Before he dropped me off he told me he would be back in three days to collect me. I was like whatever, I didn't believe him and I continued to live my life.

Three days later I was just getting home at about 7am in the morning when I opened my door and here he was sitting on my couch. I asked him what he was doing there and who let him in. He ignored me and walked into my bedroom and started packing my clothes into a bag occasionally discarding clothes he didn't like. I'm thinking this dude is "shot out" but I was actually pleased that he was there for me. I took off and never looked back. I didn't even tell my friend I was leaving. He took me to a hotel and said we had to stay there until his wife moved out of his house. I couldn't believe he was actually doing what he was saying. I remember him always on the phone talking to someone than he asked if I knew what business he was in. I knew exactly what he was involved in and I was okay with it even willing to get involved myself.

We got a phone call and he said he had to go meet someone. This time he took me with him. We went to a strip mall in Sunrise Florida and I got out of the car and was just standing on the sidewalk as he went to go talk to someone. There was this black dude standing a little ways away from me and what caught my attention was he was wearing this long trench coat and I'm thinking he's got to be hot, then I looked at his face and had to turn away because he was so disfigured. My boyfriend came back and we took off. He was upset and I asked him what was wrong. He said things didn't work out with whoever he met up with. We went back to the hotel and stayed there for another week. Much later I found out that his stepfather thought I was a cop and that black dude was there to take me out. He had a shotgun under his coat. The reason why he was disfigured was from a gunshot wound to the face. I shivered when I thought back to him. But did this stop me from going forward with this guy? Hell no! I was hooked by the danger and excitement of the fast life. I understand how that life can be enticing but it's only a dead end. Nobody makes it in that business. Eventually it catches up with you and then its game over. I moved into his house and started to learn what he was really into.

This was the early 80's and Ft. Lauderdale was booming in the drug trade. We would get a phone call and he would leave and come back with instructions to drive up to Philly or Baltimore, sometimes Gainesville or other cities. Sometimes we would run kilos up north or cash and sometimes we didn't even know what we were running. The money was good and there was always time to party when we were done. I was mainly drinking when we weren't working. It took a long time before I met his stepdad. But when I met him he saw that I was street smart and he always said he liked how I wasn't afraid of anything and he used to talk to me about certain situations asking what I thought and how would I handle it. We used to go over to my boyfriends' mothers' house every day and his stepdad was hardly ever there mainly only on holidays. He didn't bring business to the house and he was always working. I remember we used to dress the part if we were going to a certain city or a place in the country. I didn't want to draw any attention to our presence so I wanted to blend in. I used to enjoy setting up different personas for us. His stepdad would send us down to the docks sometimes to talk to the runners. We would always use codenames for the drugs we were discussing like lobster or shrimp. I kept two bags packed at all times one for cooler weather and one for hot. We were making good money but we were also blowing it just as fast. One day we got a call to drive up to Philly to pick up a car and then we were instructed to drive it to Las Vegas. We were told we were clean and we could take our time getting there. We drove straight across until we got to Denver than we took out time seeing the sights going through Utah and Arizona until we reached Vegas. To this day I still don't know why we had to drive that car out there but I learned never to ask questions. We flew back to Fort Lauderdale after staying in Vegas for a week. As soon as we got home my boyfriend said he had to go out. When he came back he told me to pack our bags we were going to

Jamaica for two weeks. He said we needed a vacation so off to Montego Bay we went. One day his dad called us and we met him at a hotel. He said he needed to get a kilo of cocaine out to Chicago real fast. He didn't want his stepson to take it. He said he would stand out more. I knew he wanted me to do it so I volunteered. Back then before 9-11 the security in the airport was very laidback so we taped it to my belly and I put on big clothes to hide the package. I was supposed to fly up with his stepdad and my boyfriend was supposed to meet us in Baltimore when we were done. I used to love doing this stuff and if there was danger involved I was even more into it. I would get so calm and I wouldn't be nervous when I was carrying.

We flew into Chicago and he made a phone call. He came back over to me and was noticeably upset. He told me to grab our bags and we went outside and got a taxi. I knew something was up because our flight to Champagne was leaving in an hour. We changed taxis three times than got tickets on a greyhound bus. We arrived in Champagne and took a taxi to the airport. I still didn't know what was going on but I followed his lead. We flew to Cincinnati and went to a hotel near the airport. He called his answering service to see if Karl had left a message. Karl wasn't where he was supposed to be and he still didn't feel comfortable so we got a ticket to Baltimore. Once there he told me that the phone call he made had informed him that we were being setup and they were supposed to bust us in Chicago. He said all was good now and I could take the package off. Well after traveling in taxis and planes in the wintertime with the heat going I couldn't get the package off because of my body sweat. It took us awhile to get the sticky tape off and I lost a little skin in the process. Shortly thereafter someone came by and took the package. My boyfriend was flying from city to city looking for us. We finally hooked up with him and I flew to Nashville and then we continued on to Ft Lauderdale. Even with that close call I still wasn't ready to give the life up and God was starting to tap on my shoulder trying to get my attention.

I thought it was time to start doing something more positive so during our down time I started going to this church down the road that helped people get their GEDs. I remember them being so nice to me and I was thinking this is how the other half lives. God was starting to reach out to me and I knew in my heart I couldn't continue going the way I was going in my life. I continued to study and eventually passed my GED test. I was very proud that I had finally accomplished something. I remember thinking I would like to have a job traveling like a flight attendant and at some point I did get a study course for it but never finished it. With our lifestyle it was hard to live any kind of a normal life and I never knew where we were going to be at any point in time. So my life continued to spiral out of control.

We used to travel a lot with his Mom and sisters. We didn't go outside of the family and he told me I couldn't have contact with any of my old friends. So we learned to do things within the family. We all used to go to different cities playing tourist visiting museums, art galleries and just seeing the sights. It was a very easy life and we had a few close calls but nothing that would make me get out of the life. This kind of life was all I was used to. I didn't know how to live any other way. I used to think about living differently but I didn't think it was possible for me. That was always for someone else so I just continued down the same path. We went back to running drugs until one day I found out that my boyfriend had found someone to replace me just like he had replaced his wife with me. I later wondered if she felt the same way that I did, shocked and betrayed. What was so bad was that I never saw it coming. I thought our relationship was perfect. He broke my heart in so many ways and I still feel pain from that relationship to this day. I had finally given my whole heart to someone and this is what happened. I've always guarded my feelings in order to protect myself but with him I left my heart wide open.

Betrayal can be a motivator and most of the time it's not a very positive one. That was my case and I was hurt so I moved out but continued to work with the family. We would still do jobs together because his stepdad didn't want his new girlfriend involved. She had just turned 18 and knew nothing about the street life. One thing I have always been was loyal so when you break that loyalty with me I don't take it very easy. I started taking a lot of the jobs by myself. I got romantically involved with stepdad but I hardly ever saw him. I saw him more to discuss a job than anything else. I had a nice place out in Tamarac, Florida and used to spend my days shopping or going to the beach. He was always traveling somewhere working and occasionally would pop in to see me or meet me to give me instructions for a job. I was starting to go outside of the family which would prove to be a big mistake for me later on or at least who I chose to associate with.

One night I got a collect phone call from him telling me he had been arrested for conspiracy to smuggle drugs. He said an FBI agent had been after him for about 15 years from when he was involved with the mob in New Jersey. This was the beginning of my downfall. I believe in Karma and I firmly think that my Karma was about to hit me tenfold. All of a sudden I didn't have any money coming in. He was locked up and couldn't give me that many jobs. Occasionally I would get one but not like I used to, so I got a job waitressing at The Inverrary Racket club near my place. He was preparing for his trial and it didn't look good. He was facing 25 years in federal prison. I remember at his trial that same pilot that we hid at the Mark 2100 club was a witness for the prosecution and he portrayed him as this big drug dealer that protected him against the Columbians. He was found guilty and sentenced to 25 years in federal prison. I remember feeling guilty because I knew something hadn't been right when he told me to meet him on the Florida turnpike and said his old friend had been calling him a lot wanting him to meet him up north because he said he had the money he had loaned him for building some storage warehouses. I think he found this odd that he finally had the money he had owed him for so long. He said he heard he was using his own product and asked me what I thought. Of course warning bells were going off in my head but for once I ignored them which I would later regret. It wasn't my fault but I blamed myself. I kept telling myself I should have said something but it was just part of the game.

The people I had started hanging out with were doing opiates and I started taking some. At first they were giving them to me but soon they started charging me for them. I started taking just Percocet for a long time. I soon found myself addicted to them and I remember I would call them wanting to buy some and they would tell me they were out. I knew they weren't they just wanted me to buy the dilaudid tablets because they could make me more money. I told them, no that I would wait till the others came in. I didn't want to start on the heavier narcotics. After a couple of days I started to get sick. I still held out and didn't call them but they called me and said they would be right over that they had something. When they got there they pulled out some syringes and some small pills that were called "dilaudid's". I told them I wasn't ready to start doing heavier drugs and I definitely didn't want to start shooting up. I can see now they were just trying to get me really hooked. I didn't give in that day but it wasn't long after that that I did give in. They could make more money off of me with the heavier drugs and that's why they stopped selling me the Percocet. They wanted me on the heavier drugs so they could support their habit by making money off of mine. Later on I would see them do the same thing with other people starting them out on the weaker stuff than cutting them off to get them to buy the more expensive and more addictive narcotics. People like that are not your friends. They are out to bring you down to their level. So I started shooting up dilaudid's and soon I had a pretty bad habit.

Because of my drug habit it soon begins to go into my living expenses. I wasn't making enough money to maintain the apartment I was living in and at that time he wasn't sending me a lot of money and the money he did send I usually blew it on pills so I moved to a duplex in Oakland Park and started selling drugs, small time in the neighborhood to try and support my habit. I ended up getting on methadone because my habit was too out of control. That's when I started hitting doctors to get narcotics. It was very easy back then. All you had to do was falsify an MRI report and you could get anything you wanted. I had a few friends who would always alter the records for me. He called me collect from prison one day and told me to go out and find three different phone booths in a small radius that would ring back when you called them. So I found three and gave him the numbers. At certain times of the day he told me to be at the payphone and wait for his call. This would trip me out because here he was in prison calling me collect and it worked. I don't know if he called me from a land line in prison or a payphone and I never asked. He always talked in code and one day he told me he needed to me to go the Miami International airport and meet a guy codename Garfield. He told me what he would be wearing and he made a point to tell me Garfield wouldn't know who was meeting him. He said his crew didn't trust this guy and he wanted me to feel him out. He said he was interested in getting some shrimp which I knew was cocaine. So I drove to the airport and went to the baggage claim where I was told he would be and sure enough there was a dude there who matched his description. As soon as I started walking towards him he looked right at me and smiled. Right then I knew he was undercover because he wasn't supposed to know who was coming so I walked right up to him and before he could say anything I asked him what time it was. The look on his face was priceless. He told me the time and I thanked him and I walked upstairs to the lounge and had a drink. I waited a while just to see if he would come into the lounge and after an hour I left and went out the same way I had come in. He was nowhere in sight so I drove back to Ft. Lauderdale and went to one of the designated payphones. He called and I told him he was right. I explained what happened and then he told me what he thought was going on. Halfway through our phone call a blue car pulled up and I recognized Garfield in the front seat. I told him he was there and he said you know what to do and I told him I would call an attorney if they wouldn't release me. I hung up the phone and Garfield and another lady got out of their car and showed me their badge. They were from the department of law enforcement, FDLE. They told me that they were taking me in for questioning and to leave my car there. They took me to their local office and placed me in a room for about an hour. I already knew they had nothing on me so I wasn't really nervous. I was actually pretty surprised I had never been brought in before after being with them for so long. This was all part of the game out in the streets. They both came in and said they were investigating the death of an undercover law enforcement agent. They explained that they had gone to Marianna Federal prison to talk to him and he wasn't very cooperative. They said in fact he wouldn't even speak to them because he said he didn't have time to talk. I had to smile to myself knowing him as I did. He could be pretty cold when he wanted to be. Garfield was really upset over that. He said he's in prison how could he not have time the time, that's all he has is time. They asked if I knew a man by the name of Darwin that was working in Gainesville and I replied I did not. I hadn't been involved in that so I knew my best bet was to act stupid and play ignorance even if I didn't know anything.

For hours they asked me questions over and over sometimes changing the questions up. They asked me what my relationship was with him and I told them that we had had a short relationship but he went to prison and I felt bad for him. I really played like a dumb blond but this blond was a brunette. I asked them if I should call my attorney that I had been cooperative by talking to them and had nothing to hide. They kept saying I wasn't under arrest and I once again asked to call my attorney. They held me there 8 hours before they finally let me go. They offered to give me a ride back to my car but I told them no thanks. I just wanted out of there. I walked out of there with my heart pumping. I called for a taxi at a payphone and went back to my car. I couldn't wait to talk to him but our next scheduled talk was for the following afternoon. The next day I got in my car and drove to the pay phone but there was a big surprise waiting for me. The look on my face was probably priceless because where the phone should be was this big hole in the ground. They had removed not only the phone but the post and wires as well. It was all gone. After the shock wore off I just had to laugh at it all. They must have really been pissed but it's all part of the game. Once again even with all of this going on I still wasn't ready to pull out. We now had to find another way to stay in contact.

The years started to pass and my addiction to pills escalated. I was self-destructing and I wasn't happy and I used to talk to my mom telling her I needed to change my life but I didn't know how and I felt trapped. Through it all my mom was always there for me no matter what I was doing she was there. I mean I had an addiction to narcotics, no job skills and the people I surrounded myself with were all drug addicts and drug dealers. I needed a change in my life but I had no idea how to pull myself out of this mess I now called my life. The contact with him would go in and out over the years but he remained a part of my life. I think he knew I was getting out of control therefore I was also dangerous.

I started living with my Mom and we moved to Wilton Manors. We rented a townhouse. I was still on methadone at the time and I started flying up to New York City to buy heroin. I used to tape it to my body like I had learned to do with him. I was never afraid to carry drugs and used to get calm when I was dirty. I had someone meet me at the airport and we would drive into Brooklyn and buy the heroin from the Dominicans. I used to take a high dose of methadone so when I tried the heroin it wouldn't hit me as hard in fact I was able to score some real potent dope that way. I had someone waiting for me back in Ft. Lauderdale and we would split the package. My partner used to fly up also so that I wasn't always seen flying up there. He proved to be my downfall. On one trip he flew up and I went to pick him up but I couldn't find him. It would be hours before I saw him and it was because the police had him and he turned on me. It wasn't long before the police raided my house.

Unfortunately because my Mom was living with me she was caught up with it all. They busted me with 69 grams of heroin and I was booked at the Broward county jail. I called my bondsman and told him what had happened and he told me he had the perfect lawyer for me. He said the lawyers' wife was running for judge and he was one of the top criminal attorneys in Ft. Lauderdale so it was a great political move. I was only in jail for about 6 hours when I was taken into the courtroom to appear before a judge. The judge assigned to my case was on vacation so Robert Trackman my attorney requested an emergency medical hearing before Judge Susan Lebow. He told the judge if I didn't get bonded out I would go into withdrawals and the county jail was not equipped to handle it. The people in the county jail had a nickname for her "let'em go

Lebow". She released me on house arrest and a half million dollar bond. My mom arranged everything with the bondsman and I returned home not long after the hearing. Our apartment was a mess. The police had rammed the door so it was hanging off the hinges. Someone came over and helped us secure the door. We were both surprised to find out they hadn't found the money I had stashed in a VHS tape. The ironic thing was it was the movie Scarface where we had hid the money. Upon going into my bedroom I saw immediately that they had also missed my biggest stash of Heroin. I had a big box of clothes where I had hid my heroin and they had taken everything out and tossed it around the room. The purse with the drugs was laying on the floor with a big footprint on it. I was back in business. I had just received a settlement from a slip and fall accident at work, Pearls Arts & Crafts. All of the money went to Robert Trackman for legal fees. He got me a plea of 2 years' probation on possession with intent.

Within a year we went back before the judge and had it terminated. I started doing fraudulent scripts and was taken in for that later on. Because of the publicity of the bust we had to move out of the townhouse and that's when I met Charlie. He had a condo for rent and we moved in there. I was back in touch with my boyfriend in prison and he started sending us money from prison. I started doing small jobs for him again. Occasionally a teamster he was involved with would come by and give me money for the phone bills which were outrageous because of all the collect calls from prison. I was very lonely and tired of answering to him all the time. He was controlling me from prison and the closer he got to getting out the worse he got. He told me he had people following me for my protection. That bothered me a lot and I started thinking if he was acting this way from prison how would it be when he got out. I was always waiting for a phone call and I was also trying to keep my habit going.

Charlie started showing me a lot of attention. I was at the point where I was ready for a change and Charlie offered that exit. He used to bring me a different car to drive every week and he was also involved in illegal activity. I started going to doctors for prescription drugs more often. There were always doctors willing to write for a price. One of the doctors was Barbara Mazzella who ended up getting busted for a pill mill. I had to write down all the pharmacy's we went to so as not to mix them up. I was still on the methadone clinic and you could always find the latest writer there from someone. After a while I ended up moving in with Charlie. Mom ended up living with my brother David. Charlie started buying me heroin and he said he could get scripts easy because of his age. This man was a trip.

He was not some fragile old man. He was very active, more so than me because of my drug use. He wanted to meet all the people that I knew that used drugs so he could start selling them pills. He was making good money off the habits of others. He saw a good way to increase his income and because he could see a lot of doctors the profit margin was big. I started out living in my own bedroom with him. I used to pick my mother up every day and we had a daily ritual of going out to breakfast. One morning I was getting ready to pick her up and he asked where I was going. I told him I was going to meet mom like usual. That's when the relationship started to change. He hit me a couple of times and said I wasn't going anywhere. I hate confrontation so I didn't go that day and I was embarrassed by what had happened and that I had done nothing about it. In the past I never would have put up with that bullshit. I was weaker now physically and emotionally.

The years of drug use had worn me down. He started to control my drug use sometimes being overly generous one day and then the next day causing me to go into withdrawals. I remember one time I flew to Chicago to detox. They put you to sleep and administer drugs to detox. When I woke up I was so sick I almost wasn't able to fly back. It did not work out well for me. Charlie had someone pick me up in a wheelchair and drive me back home. I was that sick! What was the first thing he did? He lined up dilaudid's on the floor leading to the kitchen counter where there was a syringe and spoon. I looked at him like you've got to be kidding me. I didn't go for it and I told him I wasn't starting back again so he started yelling at me calling me all kinds of names. I remember folding in on myself. It was like I couldn't even hold my body upright and I started to curl into a ball. The words had the same effect on me physically as if he was hitting me. I was curled up like I was taking blows from his fist. I still didn't get up to get the drugs so he took it to a different level. He starting slapping me across the face and pulling my hair. It was the words that got to me and broke me down. No one should be subjected to that kind of treatment. Bruises heal, but it's the mental anguish that stays with you, the loss of self-esteem that tears you down. One thing I've made a point of in my recovery is to always encourage people to better themselves and to give encouraging words. I wanted the pain to go away and it wasn't the physical pain but the mental pain. So I stood up and began to collect the pills and I saw a smile on his face which made it worse because he had won and I was weak. I asked myself how I got to this point how did it all get so badly.

There would be many times that I would stop cold turkey and be sick for days. I knew as long as I was on pills he would have control on me. He would even shoot me up when I was sleeping to get me started back on the drugs or he would put narcotics in my drinks. But what was so crazy was when I was back on them he would call me a junky and all the while he was spoon feeding me drugs. I didn't want him to have that kind of control on me and that's why I would detox all the time trying to get back some kind of control over my life. So my health continued to get worse and instead of gaining control I was losing control. I was getting weaker and weaker from the detoxing so it was messing with my mental state as well. I ended up getting doctors he didn't know about so I would have my own pills. He usually had a lot going on with the house. He was adding a bedroom onto the house so her could increase the worth on the house and resell it. He actually did all the work himself except for the electrical. There were a lot of times that Charlie would call me Tina after his granddaughter who had committed suicide. He said I reminded him of her. This troubled me a lot because this wasn't normal but it explained why he was so obsessed with me. For a while I didn't understand the obsession but now I understood and I knew I had to be careful.

Charlie had been in a nationwide trial with his daughter who he claimed was responsible for his granddaughter killing herself. He had called the police after his granddaughter was found dead with a gunshot wound to the head. His daughter had gotten a false ID for Tina and she was stripping at a club in Ft. Lauderdale underage. It became a media circus with his daughter under suspicion for Tina's death. He was on the Geraldo show and Inside Edition. They ended up making a new child abuse law called, "The Mancini law". Charlie had a book published called, "Cries from the Eagles Nest," by Ann Solomon. All of this led me to believe his relationship with his granddaughter was sexual in nature. I even used to accuse him of that and it would cause a lot of fights between us but that's what my heart was telling me. In fact it was screaming it and I knew deep down this was true. I mean you don't sleep with someone and call them by someone else's name if you don't have some feelings for them in that way.

The years went by with Charlie. Sometimes things would get so bad I would commit myself into the hospital just to get away from him. I went to one doctor to get my scripts and Charlie was so bad I walked into that office and broke down. I told him I couldn't go back to him. He told me to go straight to the hospital and he would have a room for me. I ended up staying in there for a week so drugged up I could hardly walk but it was time away from Charlie. The doctor performed all kinds of unnecessary test on me. But this would happen often that I would go to the hospital as my refuge. I used to email my best friend Nancy almost every day telling her the hell I was going through. It was a way for me to vent and it was a way to tell my story. No one should have to feel the way I did. Not any woman and that's why I'm so passionate about telling my story. I want to let other women know they are not alone out there and that there is help.

You don't have to stay in a bad relationship and the focus I want to point out is there are resources out here for women. Charlie kept me out of fear and control. He used to deprive me of sleep. He would argue with me for days and every time I would try to go to sleep he would come into the bedroom and start arguing with me then I couldn't go to sleep. The only peace I got was when he went to sleep so I would stay up just to enjoy the quietness of the house. I remember one day I was out in the carport. He had some plywood there that was left over from the room he added on in the back of the house. Charlie came out there and said he was going out for a while. I guess I didn't respond the way he wanted me to so he knocked the plywood over on top of me and left me trapped underneath it. It was too heavy for me to lift it off. I don't know how long I was stuck under there before our neighbor from next door heard me and pulled it off me. I didn't say a word I just walked into house and waited for another round. After my arrest the neighbors testified that they used to hear me screaming but no one called the police.

No one wanted to get involved. This has to stop; the silence needs to end on domestic violence. It was never ending, one story after another. At one point I tried reaching out to my ex again and I wrote him a letter in prison. I was going to ask him for help getting away from Charlie. I knew Charlie was afraid of him. A couple of weeks later the letter was returned because he had transferred somewhere else so the prison sent it back to me. Charlie just happened to get the mail that day and he read it. He was furious with me and beat me real bad that day and also hid my medicine making me sick as a punishment. I felt like giving up at that point nothing really mattered anymore and I couldn't see any way out of the relationship. I felt isolated and all alone. I really don't remember any good times between us. They may have been there but there was too much abuse to recall them. Did I love Charlie yes I did, but not in a healthy way. I know that now but at the time I loved him and put up with all of the abuse. Probably more so in the beginning but in the end all I did was fear him. I would run away and go stay with someone who was willing to help me but Charlie would either get one of the guys he worked with in the hood to come beat them up or threaten to kill one of my animals. One of my cats did end up disappearing and I don't know if he actually killed him or did something else with him. He told me he killed the cat but I was never really sure. Charlie put a tape recorder in my car and would make me sit down and listen to it accusing me of seeing someone else but all it was me making drug deals or planning my next visit to some doctor.

I learned to use payphones to talk to my mom or Nancy. I planned to fly up to VA, for almost 9 months I planned my escape from Charlie. One day I wanted till I knew he was going to be gone for a long time. I had already had a bag packed in the back of my walk-in closet so when he left I called a taxi and went to the Ft. Lauderdale airport. I flew up to Virginia and my friend Nancy and my sister Debbie picked me up at the airport. They took me to a hospital to detox and after a few days I was released but I was far from okay. These quick detoxes were taking a toll on my body.

There was nothing up there for me and my family didn't understand what I was going through. All they understood was I was a drug addict. Families can be the hardest to deal with when it comes to recovery and this is something I would like to address as I work with the youth today against drugs and violence. I still don't think they understand to this day why I just took off again and went back to Charlie. I think all they thought was I wanted to use drugs again but it was so much more than that. I was also running from my own family. It wasn't that I didn't want the help or still desired drugs it was the condescending tones and mistrust saying I needed tough love to recover. After a life on the streets when someone says you need to suffer a little more it's not something you can comprehend because the suffering has already been a part of your life so much. It was now a feeling of survival kicking in. I was tired of using drugs and tired of all the condensing words. I was tired of being looked down on by my own family. When you are weak of mind and body being told you can stay at the salvation army nightly and you have to work your way off the streets from someone who had had enough of the streets well this wasn't an option for me. I didn't know there were resources out there that could have put me in a halfway house to help me get back on my feet and could give me the support I needed. There are hotlines for battered women that you can call.

I did what I do… I ran, I took off like a jackrabbit and went back to Charlie. I know they wanted to help me but in their eyes I was just a drug addict and they were not from my world. Sadly Charlie looked more inviting then staying up in Va. with a family that didn't understand. So back to Charlie I went and right away I was back on drugs. I would even start using cocaine again which wasn't my drug of choice but Charlie was switching it up. I would later be arrested for possession and driving without a license. When I went to court for the traffic violation Charlie was so bad to me in the courtroom that I started crying and the judge Ginger-Lerner Wren called my attorney over to the side bar and asked what was going on. My lawyer knew a little about my situation and explained it briefly to the judge. They removed Charlie from the courtroom and I sat down with the judge and my lawyer. She asked if I wanted to get out of the relationship and I said I did, so she postponed my hearing and my lawyer drove me to Women in Distress in Ft. Lauderdale while the judge dealt with Charlie.

They placed me in a safe house and said victims advocate would be by to see me to help me attain a restraining order against Charlie. I waited for them to come but when they didn't show I called my lawyer and she told me to go to the courthouse and start the process myself. As soon as I walked out of the safe house Charlie was out there. I asked him how he found me and he replied it had been easy. All he had to do was stop at a store in the hood and ask the dudes standing outside the store where they kept the safe houses for battered women. They gave him directions to the place, simple! He told me to get in the car and I told him I wasn't going back. He grabbed me by the hair and he was getting very loud and I remember this guy watching us and he finally didn't like what he was seeing so he ask if there was a problem and Charlie let me go and I walked away.

I went to the courthouse and filed the restraining order against him. It even stated how he had accosted me outside the safe house. One thing I didn't know was you can fight the restraining order. That's what Charlie did. He went to court and had it dropped. So once again I ended up back with him beaten down emotionally and physically. I was very tired. I lived in a state of fear and I know the sleep deprivation was not making my state of mind any better. One night I received a phone call from a detective. She asked if Charlie was there and I replied he was. She was a detective for Ft. Lauderdale and she said a judge was looking over our case in the domestic violence court. She said some red flags came up and he had a court order for us to live in separate residences.

This was wonderful news for me and she said her and her partner would be there shortly. They got there and Charlie was outraged. He argued with them saying they couldn't do this and they had to threaten to take him to jail. They stayed there until I was packed and once I was packed I remember asking them now what and they said now you call a cab and get out of here. I felt lost and I know I wanted help at that point but I didn't know where to turn to for that help. I went to the condo that Charlie had. The one that mom and I had stayed at. It wasn't long before Charlie showed up and I called the police like they told me to do when he broke the restraining order. By the time they got there Charlie would be gone and then they would get on me about calling. This was crazy to me, here they are supposed to be keeping us apart and they are getting mad at me. This was the last time that I tried leaving. I went back to him because he had cut off all my resources and I had no food or money which meant I also didn't have any drugs.

I was in a bad place. I've learned this is all part of the abuse isolation, low self-confidence, a feeling of helplessness. I don't want to see women go down the same path I did. I had sold drugs prostituted myself and ended up living in total darkness. I would be with Charlie for almost seven years. My physical condition was weakening from drug use and constantly going through withdrawals. I was up and down emotionally and I was also developing a fear to even leave the house. I contemplated suicide many times. I wasn't sleeping and when I would try to go to sleep Charlie would come into the bedroom and start arguing with me until I gave up trying to sleep. The name calling was getting worse those last two days and he was constantly grabbing me by the hair or shoving me against the walls. I was having migraines all the time and I was going to the emergency room frequently for them.

The stress was becoming unbearable. The day it happened I went into the bedroom to get some rest. As soon as I started to fall asleep Charlie walked in there started yelling at me and grabbed me by the hair and dragged me through the kitchen into a spare bedroom we used for an office. There was a kitchen knife on the desk and he grabbed it and put it up against my throat. He said he was going to cut my F---ing throat. By that time I was just tired and over the whole thing. I told him to go ahead and he just yelled some more and I went back to bed. A short time later he came back into the bedroom and he was in a rage. He grabbed me by the hair again and dragged me once more through the house. This time I knew he was going to kill me. I was in a state of fear and when we reached the bedroom I grabbed the knife this time and started stabbing him. All I knew was I had to kill him or he was going to kill me. I snapped and all the fear and rage I had been feeling for all these years came out. For years I had taken all the abuse without fighting back. Years later I would be reading through the transcripts and I would come to the deposition my mom did and her words would stay with me for years and help me understand what and why it happened. She told the prosecutor and my attorney that she could never understand why I didn't fight back when we fought. She said I just took it. I wouldn't even argue back I would just take it. After it was over I was in a state of shock and couldn't believe what I had done.

We had a safe in the office where we kept all our prescriptions and a notepad with the names of the doctors we both went to. I was hysterical and in a panic. I started grabbing pill bottles and I was taking pills as fast as I could. Pills were going all over the floor and I grabbed a bottle of dilaudid's and went into the kitchen and started shooting up as many as I could. I remember calling my mom and telling her I had gone to the store and had come home and found Charlie dead. She told me to get out of the house. She couldn't figure out how I had gone to the store because Charlie never let me out of his sight or let me go anywhere. Eventually I told her the truth about what happened. I still couldn't understand how I could have killed him. I didn't want to believe I could have done such a thing. That's why I kept making up a different story about what really happened. I finally told her the truth and she told me to call the police. I told her not to worry that I had taken off my bloody clothes and left them in the room and had not disturbed the crime scene so the police would see what had really happened. Charlie still had a clump of my hair in his hand from dragging me through the house. I called Nancy and told her that Charlie was dead and that I found him after coming back from the store. I was telling everybody the same story. I was still taking drugs and was very suicidal. I just wanted to be left alone so I could die but my tolerance was so high and the adrenaline was racing through my body.

I was just so very tired of the life I had been living. I wasn't living that was the whole point. I knew my life was complete darkness and suffering. I firmly believe God kept me alive that day because he had a plan for me. There was no way I should have been alive after taking all the drugs I did that day. Nancy called my sister and told her the story about me finding Charlie and she told her I was suicidal. My sister called the police and told them I had found Charlie and that I was in the house with Charlie and I was trying to OD on pills. The police were sent out to our house and I told them Charlie wasn't there. I just wanted to be left alone. I remember finally just giving up. I couldn't take it anymore. I just wanted them to go away so I could OD. But I finally gave up and allowed them to come in to our house. I was placed in the police car while they investigated the scene. Then I was taken to the police station where they started questioning me. I confessed to killing him. From that point on I always took responsibility for killing him. What surprised me was the police said I killed him over the drugs because the pills were all over the floor but that was from me in a panic dropping them all over the place. Yes Charlie had spoon fed me drugs, had me up and down but that night I wasn't in withdrawal. I was taken to the hospital because they believed I had had a stroke. I was then placed in the infirmary at the Broward county jail.

I wouldn't eat or talk to anyone and I went into withdrawals real bad. I got down to 80lbs and when the nurses told me if I didn't start eating they were going to force feed me so I started eating. The only person I would talk to in the beginning was my attorney. I was in shock and unrecognizable. I was in a wheelchair because I was too weak to walk. I didn't want to talk to anyone. I just wanted to be left alone and I wasn't ready to deal with what had happened.

I firmly believe God doesn't give you more than you can handle and God was giving me the time I needed to become stronger so that I could face what was coming. He would continue to work in my life throughout the years. Eventually they put me in a maximum security cell at the Pompano detention center. I would end up staying in the county jail for about 2 and a half years before I took a plea of 2nd degree murder. They charged me with 1st degree murder and I was facing the death penalty. This was serious and I don't know if I really comprehended just how much trouble I was in. I mean yes I knew I was facing a lot of time but it was also possible that I would never get out of prison or get the death penalty. That was a very scary thought. I knew I didn't premeditate Charlie's murder I just snapped when he dragged me through the house and all the pain and abuse I had endured with him and with others finally came out and I was finally done with taking the abuse. I was finally standing up for myself saying no more, no more pain, no more fear and no more humiliation. But the state was saying I killed him over drugs and I guess in a sense that was exactly what I had done. If I hadn't been hooked on drugs I wouldn't have most likely been there with him. But there was so much more to my case than a woman addicted to drugs.

I was a woman who had been traumatized as a young child countless times and had been in a lot of abusive relationships. Charlie played a game with me by using the drugs as a form of control by having me dependent on him for the next fix. He used to also like making me sick than nursing me back to health. It was the power he had over me that he liked, the total dependence I had on him. This was a time bomb just waiting to explode. My guilt was so bad that I thought I deserved everything I got. If they had offered me life instead of 15 years I would have accepted it. I had a great legal team and my lawyer George Reres fought for me and went to the state showing them along with a team of psychologists the abuse I had suffered throughout the years.

George was a public defender with Broward County and specialized in death penalty and homicide cases. He put together a dream team for me that would save my life. We filed a Notice of Intention to rely upon the Defense of Battered Spouse Syndrome. I had four expert witnesses to show such battered spouse syndrome; Dr. Lenore Walker, Dr. Sherri Bourg-Carter, Dr. David Shapiro, and Dr. Meryl Rome MD. Dr. Lenore Walker had been a pioneer in the field of domestic violence in her private practice as well as at the state, national, and international level. She is a licensed psychologist and founded the Domestic Violence Institute. She has been in the national and local media discussing issues around domestic violence, introduction of the Battered Woman Syndrome in self-defense cases where women killed their abusive partners and drew attention for her work with the O.J. Simpson defense team. A frequent guest on popular television shows, she was featured on a Court TV segment and interviewed for 48 Hours. She would spend hours evaluating me and doing countless testing on my mental state. She found I suffered from battered woman's syndrome. I had Dr. Sherri Bourg-Carter a forensic psychologist with expertise in criminal, civil, and family psycho-legal matter. Some of her high profile cases were Aileen Wournos, (serial killer), Lionel Tate, (child killer), Jacqueline Reynolds, (killed her mother), Amy Weis, (infanticide), and Kenneth Wilk, (cop killer). She is a forensic consultant on homicide, domestic violence, and death penalty cases. Dr. Carter usually was an expert for the prosecution so it was wonderful news to know she would be on my side. Then I had Dr. Shapiro who is one of America's most respected forensic psychologists, being one of the first psychologist to apply clinical principles of assessment and diagnosis to the criminal and civil courtroom, and is a consultant on criminal cases on topics that include assessment of competency, criminal responsibility, death penalty, neuropsychological screenings, and assessment of post-traumatic stress disorders. Then I had Dr. Meryl Rome a psychologist in Boca Raton Florida evaluating me. We also had an investigative team who did research for George and Dr. Walker had a lot of interns come in to work with me doing testing and therapy.

George now had my dream team put together and they would put together a defense to show my state of mind at the time of offense, evaluations of competency which would include evaluations of competency to stand trial and competency to waive Miranda rights and competency to confess, plus risk assessment of the potential for future violence and defense of battered woman's syndrome. There are four general characteristics of the syndrome.

1. The woman believes that the violence was her fault.

2. The woman has an inability to place the responsibility for the violence elsewhere.

3. The woman fears for her life.

4. The woman has an irrational belief that the abuser is omnipresent and omniscient.

An abused woman has to overcome feeling inadequacy, crazy, or stupid- something akin to brainwashing- as a result of having been repeatedly told she was these things while in the relationship. I could call George anytime and tell him I needed to see him and he would say I'll be right over. He never told me he was too busy or didn't have time for me. They were worried I wasn't strong enough to go through a trial. I might have been healing physically but my emotional state was very fragile.

When we were going to pre-trial hearings I wasn't holding up very well. The trauma I had suffered throughout the years had come to an end. I wanted help and George was reaching out to me offering that help I so desperately needed. All my life I had been counted out as a drug addict but George saw beyond that. He just saw a woman that needed help and direction and definitely a positive influence. I had been surrounded by negativity on the streets so long that this was like a lifeline for me to hold onto. I finally saw some hope in my future and I wasn't letting go. I knew God was working in my life and he had brought someone in my life who would not lead me astray. Without a doubt I would have gotten life if they hadn't believed in me so much and worked so hard on my defense. What George was doing was ultimately giving me a second chance at life when everybody else had counted me out.

The power of having someone believe in you is remarkable and can change even the hardest person. Sometimes that's all it takes is just that one person and then everything changes. A whole new world opens up. George was that one person who changed my life in the very beginning and there were countless others throughout the years that helped me become the person I am today. What really came as a surprise to me was when I was in courtroom accepting the plea, Debra Zimmet; the state prosecutor came over to me after it was over and offered me her hand saying she wished me luck in my future. I remember feeling very taken back that she was actually wishing me well and George told me she had felt bad about my case. This showed me that George had gone above and beyond in showing the state not only my background but what had happened and why I had killed Charlie.

I would do the time and I was ready to move forward even though I was scared about going to prison. I heard all kinds of stories about prison and how bad it was. I remember the girls talking about one guard Ms. Pringle and how bad she was. I even started to have dreams about the lady. I had been in the county jail for almost two years in a maximum security two man cell and the thought of having a little bit of freedom was something to look forward to even if it was prison it had to be better than where I was at. My dreams were very troubled and I would have nightmares every night.

I was on so much medication in the county jail and I wasn't functioning very well. I had one reoccurring nightmare that haunted me almost nightly. It would always be the same. A man would have me tied to a table and while I watched he would slice my legs with a knife. I would have cuts all over and I would wake up screaming. It would be years before my nightmares stopped. My lawyer contacted Dr. Lenore Walker and told her about my nightmares and the problems I was having. She had an intern come to the county jail to talk to me and try to help me work through my nightmares. Her name was Susanna and she really helped me through a rough time. It was nice just being able to talk to someone who genuinely cared and actually listened.

We went over my past and for the first time I told everything that had ever happened to me. Sharing my past was difficult for me but it was also the beginning of the healing process. I had always been judged for my past so it was a new experience for me. I was talking to my brother on the phone while I was in the county jail but those calls soon started to get less frequent. It hurt me because we had always been so close but now there was a wall between us. Once I got sentenced he no longer wanted to talk to me. I never heard from him again and he stopped taking my calls.

A week after being sentenced I was transferred to Broward reception facility where I went through R&O. I was stripped search, yelled at, and then they gave me a DC number. From now on I would be just a number not Donna Buchanan but a six digit number. I felt belittled and violated as everything was stripped away from me. I had to gather all my strength and through God's grace I was able to stand tall and face the nightmare that had become my life. Then after hours of standing around in a towel I was given a uniform and a bedroll. We had to walk through the whole compound to our dorm. I remember women yelling at us as we walked and how everyone had walked out of their dorms to see who the new people were. I felt like I was on display. While I was in the county jail one of the girls told me to never show them that you are weak. I always remembered that and it would help me survive all the years I spent inside. We couldn't make phone calls so there was no contact from the outside. Luckily I only stayed in that dorm for two weeks before I was placed into general population.

Now it was time to learn how to survive in prison. My first job was in the kitchen and it was hard work being woken up at 2:30 A.M. and getting used to the routine there. Being new you were assigned the worse jobs and you had to do more than the girls who had been there awhile. I also noticed that the COs also treated the new girls differently. I was written up so many times my first year. You couldn't talk if you were in a line and sometimes I would be looking the other way and I would get written up. You could at times work extra duty to get the CC's they wrote taken off your record and I found myself volunteering a lot in the beginning. I told my mom that I could do the 15 years but what I couldn't handle was losing her while I was in.

My mother is the one who gave me strength and the courage to change my life. She never gave up on me and was always there. She always believed in me and encouraged me to change my life but she never pushed me just prayed for me and let God work in my life. My mom means the world to me and I thank God for her every day. I had no clue what it would be like in prison and what I would need. I remember my first week in prison I received a money order from my mom and I was like how did she know. I wouldn't have asked for it but mom knew. She was for real and she had her baby girls back. Prison does not provide everything you need. They have a canteen and if you don't get family or friend support you go without. Just even the necessities of shampoo and conditioner, it all cost's money. Mom made sure I had everything I needed and I didn't have to go hungry. Prison food is exactly as bad as everyone says it is and with the economy as bad as it is, that has affected the quality and quantity of the food you receive.

When you are in prison it feels like everyone has forgotten you. At first they accept your collect phone calls but after a while that stops. Mail is a very big thing in prison and everyone would stand around at night and wait for the mail to be given out in hopes of hearing something from the outside. I would see the hope on the girl's faces and then see it fall. Sometimes the girls would receive bad news about their families and the pain I saw would break my heart. I was always very protective of the young ones so I would reach out to them. These girls were from the streets from the only life I had come to know and I wanted even then to put a stop to all the drugs and violence. But I still had change to do in my life. If you are weak then you are a victim and they will prey on that. I see so many girls in there with no support. Visitation is the second biggest thing in prison hoping to hear your name called. After a while I used to talk to the new girls that came in and didn't have anything and show them how to make some money so that they could take care of themselves.

Change did not come quickly it took years with the help of a lot of people before that would happen. I knew I wanted life to be different but my old habits and the people I always had associated with were still there.

After a few months I was transferred to Homestead Correctional Institution. It was a maximum security prison and most of the inmates were serving 15 years to life. I remember my first day there a fight broke out and the guard locked the doors and watched it happen. I was like wow I'm really in prison now. This is where I'll be for 15 years. You have to be careful who you hang around with because they let you see what they want you to see not who they really are. I know at Homestead you never asked what you were in for. There were so many that had life sentences there. The high profile cases were usually known but I learned not to ask questions about your time or crime. They had two man cells and my first bunky was a very Young girl named Mone. We would become very close throughout the years. She was only 20 and was serving a 20 year mandatory sentence and that is too young to be doing so much time. We used to get in all kinds of trouble together hustling food out of the kitchen to selling contraband on the compound. If there was money to be made Mone' would find it.

I started going to school to get my TABE scores up and that's when I first learned I was good at teaching the other girls math and English. I was only enrolled in school for a short time because my grades were too high. So I started working at Rec and there was one guard who saw something in me and reached out to me. I doubt she even knows to this day how much of an impact she had on my life. Her name was Ms. Garcia and she would talk to me often. She saw that I was with the wrong crowd but she never wrote me up even when I was caught red handed. She would just say Donna you got to be slicker than that and I used to kick myself when she did that. She told me if I hung around a bad crowd I would be grouped in with them. I told her I wasn't doing anything and they were my friends. I still didn't understand that if you associate yourself with the wrong crowd you associate yourself with negativity and sooner later you are going to start doing the wrong things and making wrong choices.

Of course soon I found myself involved in doing the wrong things and making the same bad choices that I had on the outside. Through it all Ms. Garcia continued to talk to me and I kept asking myself why is she trying so hard because I still had 12 years left to do and I didn't care whether I got in trouble because I had more than enough time to make it up. But then I had to ask myself if she saw something then there must be something there.

Once again God was tapping on my shoulder trying to lead me in the right direction. I was becoming aware and slowly I was making a change. It might have been a small one but one nonetheless. Homestead would be a learning place for me and later I would look back on it and see where my frame of mind was. Ms. Garcia got me a job working canteen. Once again she was trying to help me. The canteen job was a very sweet job there and it was the only paying job in prison with only three positions available. So it was very hard to get a job there. She was always giving me advice because it was so easy to get involved with the wrong things. She would tell me if I was doing something wrong so that I didn't lose my position. But I was already doing the wrong thing. I started fronting out canteen, two for oneing where someone would want to buy a $100.00 of canteen and the next week they would have to pay me $200.00. I was the canteen person to go to if you needed something. I ended up going to the hole for 60 days for bartering for something I wasn't even doing as well as an investigation. That doesn't mean I was innocent in the game I had just gotten in trouble for someone else's wrong.

It was very rough and I wrote my sister a letter venting to her about my treatment. I mean you don't get many privileges in lock up but the ones you do get were being denied to me. She wrote the governor and said my rights were being violated. By this time I had just gotten out after doing 60 days. They investigated and found this to be true so I was back in the hole for another 30 days to await transfer to a different institution per review after being out only three days. They woke me up at 3:30 A.M. and I was transferred to Broward Correctional and placed in the hole there for a day and then they drove me to Lowell Correctional and I went back into the hole. Two days later they drove me to Gadsden Correctional Institution and placed me in general population. Gadsden was a private facility run by CCA and was a minimum security prison. It wasn't like Homestead; it was mainly short timers with a few years to do, so the mindset was different. At first I hated it and I was angry that I had left Homestead. It was also a closed compound which meant you couldn't go out in the yard. I was used to Homestead where you could just walk out of your dorm and go outside. I thought Gadsden was a Mickey Mouse compound totally different than Homestead. The place was nicknamed camp cupcake and after doing time in a maximum security prison I guess it was.

Every place has its cliques and Gadsden was no different. I could go two ways, the way I had been going or try a new way. The old way surely wasn't working and I thought nobody knows me here, not like at Homestead. My case was pretty high profile so everyone knew what I was in for at Homestead but here at Gadsden nobody knew me. It was 30 miles from Tallahassee so I hadn't been news there. I started to look around to see what kind of place it really was. I've always just sat back and watched to see what kind of game was being played just like on the streets before I got involved in something. What I saw was this, it was no different than any other compound when it comes to the drugs and hustling and it was probably worse because there was a lot of corruption from within. Girls were getting all kinds of things mailed in to them because the mailroom was a joke. You could pay off officers to bring you in whatever you wanted. Later there would be a lot of arrest of officers and they would bring the place under control again. So here I was at a crossroad, do I try something new or try something else. The answer seemed obvious to me, hell yes! I try something different. I would be a fool to think I could continue following my old ways and make something out of myself. Here I could be anybody I wanted to be, a fresh start.

I was 43 years old and it was time to grow up. I became a teacher's aide and was LVA certified to help the girls get their GED. I began tutoring in the dorm and at school. Math and Algebra was my favorite subject's so that's what I usually helped the girls with. It was a good feeling to have someone run up to me all excited because they had just passed their GED test and they wanted to thank me. That felt wonderful to see how much it meant to these girls to achieve something.

This was a very good time for me. I liked seeing other people accomplish something on their own. So I was always encouraging all the new girls to get into class. This is when I started to learn I was very good with the young girls. I mean there wasn't anything they could tell me that I hadn't heard or hadn't done myself. I was also very careful not to make them feel bad about their past but to say okay you did that and you did this but the question is now what are you going to do about it. How are you going to change your life for the better? A lot of times they just needed someone to listen to them. I used to go to Recreation and watch the girls training the dogs. They had an honor dorm for the dogs so I went to Ms. Conrad and asked to be moved into the dorm. I waited 6 months before I was finally moved there. It was a totally different atmosphere than the general population. In the general population there were no rules to follow in the dorm except what the CO's tell you to do. I think the noise used to get to me more than anything.

You have 71 women in one dorm yelling and fights were always breaking out. But in the dog dorm there was some kind of control and there were rules in the dorm that you had to follow or you would be moved back to the general population. That's not to say it was perfect or that things didn't happen in there, just not as often. Living in the dog dorm I was able to watch them as they trained. This is how I started to learn dog training and I knew I wanted to do this. After about a year I was accepted into a vocational class called Auto CAD. I remember I was so excited about this class because this would be the first time I had ever done something really positive with my life. I mean I had been helping others but what had I really done myself. I always believe in doing something myself before asking someone else to do it.

My teacher was Ms. Knorp and she would be such a positive influence on not only me but everyone else in that class. She believed in us and always encouraged us to make something out of our life. Let me tell you this lady was out of her element. Here she was an architect, a real nerd and she was trying to teach girls college level when most of us hadn't even graduated from high school. You had to give this lady Kudos for teaching us. It was rough in the beginning. It was the first class and we didn't even get computers for a few months so it was math, math, and math. We were all getting stressed out and she was trying to figure out how to connect with us. This was the first time she had worked inside the prison system and we knew she was naïve. But let me tell you this lady was tough. We even made her cry a few times but she hung in there with us and made sure everyone of her girls made it to graduation.

I started getting involved with the fundraising at Gadsden. Every year we would have an annual heart walk and raise money. One year we reached $11,000. That was impressive considering we raised it from prison. We also raised money for the cancer society, literary society and relay for life.

In the fall of 2008 I was contacted by Burrud productions asking if I would tell my story on a Show called Women Behind Bars on Wetv. I thought here was a chance for me to not only tell my story but to also take full responsibility for what I had done. I wrote them back and agreed to do it. They filmed me at Gadsden and they flew up north to see my family and interview them as well. It would be a long time before I would see the show. To prepare for the show I felt I needed to see all the depositions and review my case so I requested these documents from my lawyer George Reres. This gave me a chance to understand what and why it happened and since it had been 8 years I could look at it through different eyes. It would be another step in the healing process and helped me face what had happened.

Dealing with my past has been the hardest part for me. I always ran away from the pain not willing to face it but it was time to come to terms with what had happened in my life. Just as I had learned with the dogs once you face your fears you can then move forward. Girls always tell me they are ashamed of their past and they are afraid to share it, but this is how I see it. The past is just that... the past and if you are doing something positive in your future and making a difference people are going to notice that more than what you did in the past. It's what you are doing now that counts.

I think prison taught me not to care what people thought of me and said about me and to just be my own person. There's so much anger and pain inside and a lot of the women try to hurt you and will say a lot of hurtful things so you either learn to get past what they say or it will break you down. I refused to be torn down because I had too many years of abuse and not standing up for myself and I refused to be weak again. My self-confidence was building in myself. I don't regret doing the show at all. I was able to share what had happened to me and hopefully helped someone else and bring closure to Charlie's family. I wanted to let women know they are not alone and it was the beginning of me educating others that there is only prison or death out in the streets.

God was building a foundation for my life and future. He had a plan for me and this was just the start of something bigger something I didn't even know I was headed for in my future. He was slowly working in my life and my thinking was changing. I graduated Auto CAD two years later and was certified as a drafting assistant and blueprint reader. While I had been in Auto CAD I had tried out for the CCI dog team three times. I wasn't picked each time so I asked Ms. Conrad why I didn't make it and what could I do next time to do better. She told me that it was my lack of self-confidence and working with dogs you have to be assertive. What I lacked in self-confidence I made up in persistence. I wanted to be a part of the dog program so I continued to try out. In 2009 a new dog program came to Gadsden.

Beverly Sebastian with the national greyhound foundation had a program called Second Chance at Life. It was the brainstorm of a couple of filmmakers who once used to make low-budget movies in Hollywood. Before the dogs came along, Beverly Sebastian, 77, and husband Ferd, 79, were making a living on drive-in titles such as "Rocktober Blood," "Delta Fox." Gator Bait," "American Angels: Baptism of Blood," and their last, a biker flick called "Running Cool." In 1993 the Sebastian's moved to Florida on the intent of producing a feature film on greyhound racing and instead fell in love with the greyhounds. The deeper they looked into the racing industry the worse it got. Greyhounds are bred to sprint at hunting speeds of up to 45 mph - second only to the cheetah. They fell in love with their mellow dispositions. The Humane Society once put the number of racing greyhounds being euthanized, abandoned, or sold to medical facilities at 40,000 annually. In 1994 Beverly and Ferd Sebastian responded by starting The National Greyhound Foundation which is a non- profit group. So far they have placed approximately 7,000 dogs with families across the nation. But the adoptions take time so in 2006 they approached the prison systems for help.

They called it Second Chance at Life. The volunteer inmates would feed and groom the dogs and teach them obedience training along with working on behavioral problems. The best and brightest would be trained for therapy and service dogs. In 2012 they started the Purple Heart greyhound program and the advanced dogs would be trained to assist veterans with PSTD. Together with the inmates this would become a win-win situation. This program would teach the inmates positive behavior and positive change. This would be the first time that most of these women would ever experience unconditional love. Together with the inmates they would begin to change the lives of not only the retired greyhounds but the lives of inmates. Right before I graduated Auto CAD this time I was chosen to be a part of Second Chance at Life. Not only was I chosen but Ms. Conrad chose me as a dog handler. Nobody had ever worked with greyhounds there so it was a very exciting time for us and a great opportunity to do something positive with my life. Gadsden had three dog programs now; CCI, Easter Seal and now Second Chance at Life. My first greyhound dog was named Alex. We were all able to name our own dogs. I met Beverly and Ferd Sebastian and was instantly impressed with what they were doing. It was a

Christian program and their enthusiasm for the greyhounds and the inmates was so passionate

I soon became just as passionate for the program myself. I had so much to learn about training dogs. A lot of the greyhounds came in with behavioral problems and I started reading dog training books and books on behavioral problems. I became an avid fan of Cesar Milan. Ms. Conrad had DVDs we could watch of not only Cesar but Victoria Stillwell. I would spend hours watching those videos learning all I could from them. I still hadn't come to terms with my past life fully and definitely hadn't forgiven myself totally for what I had done. I started signing up for betterment classes and domestic violence classes. I joined women helping women and some art therapy classes for domestic violence.

I had been writing George Reres over the years keeping him informed on what I had been doing while in prison. He wrote me a letter August 27, 2009 saying it was great to hear that I was motivated to change my life and help other battered women there at Gadsden. He said it must be exciting and scary all at once when I consider that I will be released soon. He said it seemed to him that I had always been the hardest on myself and that it could just as easily been him defending Charlie for killing me. He said I needed to forgive myself so that I could move on. I always kept that letter and when I started to doubt myself or question if I was doing the right thing I would pull that letter out and read it again. This letter touched me very deeply and I will forever be grateful to George for taking the time out to write to me and try to continue to help me. His job was done when I took the plea but he continued to care. This is when I said to myself that in order to change I had to forgive myself so that I could move forward. When you forgive yourself you can also begin to forgive others but it starts within you. By moving forward I could also begin to help others. I actually learned that concept from training dogs and watching Cesar Milan. Cesar always talks about how the dogs don't stay in the past it's usually the humans that can't move forward and his concept helped me understand what I needed to do.

Being a part of a team and working with others was new for me but it was a learning experience that showed me how to take constructive criticism and patience. I had never been a part of something other than the street trade. It felt good! As the time went by my confidence grew and my training kept getting better. I began to notice that there were so many young girls in there with no family support and no positive influences in their life.

I started encouraging the girls to start wellness classes and vocational classes. Not only should you use your mind but your health and well-being is also very important to make a positive balance. Just like Cesar talks about well balance with the dogs the same can be true with humans. I had also begun to take exercise classes and I could immediately see a change in not only my body but my mind. I couldn't tell somebody else to do something if I wasn't willing to do it too.

Soon I was an aide for step aerobics class with my friend Perez who would be my mentor teaching me how to be a dog whisperer and together we would promote wellness in a big way. Just a kind word in a place that wasn't always kind went a long way. There were so many girls there involved with wellness Tyson, Mistie, Jamie, Jackie, Welkner and countless others.

I continued in the dog program and grew as a person myself. I remember growing up around dogs and they were always a part of my life. I felt like I had come full circle and I was becoming the person I was meant to be. I was becoming a leader teaching the other girls how to train the greyhounds and after being on the team a couple of years I was chosen to be team leader along with another girl named Dixie. I always had a problem standing up in front of a crowd speaking but when I talked about my passion it all came so easily. I no longer felt nervous and I was able to share my love and knowledge for the dogs. We would do circle training and I put together some training videos and taught training techniques and how to handle behavioral problems. I really enjoyed working with the dogs. I always felt so good when I was around them and they never failed to bring a smile to my face. At times it was very rough inside but I refused to let it change me for the worse.

I would always tell people do your time don't let your time do you. It's what you make of it. There was one girl that really made an impact on my life. Her name was Angela McDonald and when I met her she was a law clerk. She had tried out for the dog team a few times and I could see a passion inside of her. She started the biggest loser program and lost an impressive amount of weight. She was chosen as a dog handler and become a full time dog handler. She was always willing to drop whatever she was doing in order to help someone else.

The reason I'm telling this story is because sometimes when you come in you don't always get that second chance to come out. Gods plan was for her to come home, so on March 24, 2011, at 7:00 A.M. Angela McDonald died in prison. Her loss affected so many people there not only inmates but countless staff as well. We had a memorial service for her and planted a tree in her honor. A year from the day she died that plant started to bud and we knew that Angie was still with us. Angie would always be in our hearts and not forgotten for all her many accomplishments while in prison and for those she helped.

This also reminded me how God had given me a second chance so I wanted to make my life count for something. I have seen quite a few women die in prison while I was inside never getting that second chance to come out. God has chosen me to be one of his soldiers to go out in the street to share his message and to give back. After a couple of years Beverly and Ferd told us they were starting a new dog program called the Purple Heart Greyhound program. Senior handlers were picked to start training the greyhounds for service dogs for veterans with post-traumatic stress disorder (PTSD). To be able to give back and help someone from prison was a wonderful feeling. Being inside always makes you feel helpless but here was a way I could help someone who was fighting for our country. I became totally involved with the program and became a full time dog handler. I had already trained 15 dogs for obedience training to be adopted as pets.

January 18, 2012 Beverly and Ferd brought an 18 month old fawn greyhound who I named Falcor to be one of the first Purple Heart greyhounds trained for service. Falcor's name had special meaning for me and so I named him after the dog dragon in The Neverending Story. Falcor was on a quest and so was I. Together we would work to make an impact on other people's lives. He was a big 80 pound fawn greyhound who loved to socialize and would smile and show his front teeth when he greeted you. We had four greys training for service, Sox, Brix, Nickel and Falcor.

I first began his obedience training with the help of my co-handler Cassy Callahan. She was new to the program but a wonderful student who was willing to take constructive criticism. Once Falcor had learned all his obedience training we started teaching him advanced commands. We taught nudge where he is taught to wake the vet who is having a nightmare or encourage a depressed vet to get up out of bed or off the couch. The dog is expected to keep nudging the vet until the "enough" command is given. Another important command was circle. A lot of vets have trouble being in crowds so with the circle command you can make a small circular movement with your hand and the dog will circle around the vet giving him space from the crowd. I would train my service dogs to retrieve medicine bottles so if the vet was having an anxiety attack and was frozen the dog could bring it to them. I also taught them to turn light switches on and off and to open doors. Once the advanced training was finished then Falcor would leave to do his public access training on the outside. It was always hard saying goodbye to the dogs but knowing they were going to a good home and would be helping someone made it worthwhile. Falcor left on June 7, 2013 to begin his public access training. Falcor passed his public access training. Joann and Ken Weulfling would work with Falcor and his new recipient Army Nurse veteran Leisel. Three newspapers The Gadsden County times, Sarasota Herald Tribune, and the Chronicle would interview the dog program at Gadsden. I would even be on the Tallahassee WCTV channel six news talking about the Purple Heart greyhound program. Now I could see that I can help other people and also be a positive influence and with this knowledge comes more confidence in myself. My dream begins to blossom and once more I knew I was on the right path and this is what I was meant to do with my life.

On July 4, 2012 Rob and Lucinda Boyd reached out to me in prison after seeing my documentary on Wetv. I remember getting this package in the mail and pulling out a photograph of a man. I didn't have my glasses on and I asked Virginia, "Who sent me a picture of Stevie Wonder?" She laughed at me and told me to put my glasses on. I then had to laugh because it definitely wasn't a picture of Stevie Wonder but of Rob Boyd with The Streets Don't Love You Back Movement. I started reading the letter he sent me and he told me him and his wife had seen my show on Wetv," Women Behind Bars" and my story was so powerful that they decided to reach out to me in prison and tell me about their movement, The Streets Don't Love You Back.

After being on the streets all my life and knowing this, it had a profound effect on me. I wouldn't know then that I would become a member of their movement and would later go on to educate the youth today against drugs and violence and domestic violence. I read about everything they were doing and I said to myself now here are some people that are giving back to society in a big way. I was very impressed with what I saw and it made me feel good that my show had actually reached out to someone. That was one of the reasons I had done it and God was slowly moving me down the path I needed to go.

On July 9, 2012 Beverly and Ferd brought a whole entourage to Gadsden. Two reporters from the Sarasota Herald Tribune joined them and I was able to meet Army nurse Leisel and her daughter and work with them together showing the commands that I had taught Falcor. Warden Molina and Ms. Norris set up a luncheon down at Rec and I'm thinking to myself am I really in prison. I had to check myself because I was thinking this couldn't be prison. Where does this happen and how often does this opportunity come to someone serving a 15 year sentence for 2nd degree murder. Warden Molina and Ms. Norris believed in us girls and they are responsible for changing girls lives in there with their support and encouragement that you can do something with your life even if you are incarcerated. The reporters interviewed the whole dog team then everyone sat down for lunch where Ferd blessed our food and we had a great lunch. After lunch they released all the other girls and Beverly me pulled me aside and with a smile on her face said the whole afternoon was planned for the veteran, her daughter and I.

I was so excited and it was probably one of my greatest moments in prison. I would sit down with them and go over Falcors' commands showing her how I did them and answering any questions she might have. This was such an honor for me. I have never felt so proud so inspired and what was really wonderful is I felt total confidence because this is what I knew, this was my passion and I was confident in my knowledge on dog training. Beverly and Ferd filmed us at the visitation park along with the two reporters for their documentary. I remember the CO's teased me afterwards asking me for my autograph. It was an amazing moment in my life. A few months went by and I was working on my second service dog who I named Atreyu after the Indian in The Neverending Story. Atreyu was an extraordinary dog. He was only two years old and had the best disposition. Beverly had handpicked him for me and said she thought he would be outstanding for service. Within five weeks Atreyu already knew all his basic commands and most of his advanced commands. I used to take him into the chow hall as part of his training. I would give him the "Under" command and he would go under the table and stay there until I released him. It usually takes at least 10 weeks or more before they are trained enough to do this command but Atreyu was doing it in 5 weeks. There were two officers at Gadsden that interacted a lot with the dogs and the inmates. Their names were Sgt. Harper and Officer Giannini. A lot of the greyhounds lacked socialization and most were afraid of the CO's and Sgt. Harper and Officer Giannini often worked with them walking them around or giving those commands or treats to make it a positive experience. Right away Atreyu fell in love with them. He would get so excited when he saw them and that's the only time he would break his commands. I would be in the chow hall and he would get up from under the table and I instantly knew one of them was around. I would look around and sure enough I would see one of them. They would laugh and swear they didn't look at him. Mr. Giannini would come down to rec to see Atreyu or come in the dorm to visit with him. He became so fond of him he adopted him but ended up having to give him up because of a previous dog in the house didn't get along with Atreyu. There are a few officers at Gadsden that I have to commend for their positive influences and not seeing us as just inmates. I learned I could also make an influence over not only the girl but those around me. A lot of the CO's become very cold to the girls inside but I would talk to them and encourage them also to get an education and better their lives. Mr. Giannini is now going to nursing school.

We must always remember that our actions can also affect others and serve as an example. When someone sees you achieving something in life it makes them want to also succeed. Gadsden had changed over from CCA to MTC and the new warden Mr. Sergio Molina believed in preparing the girls for reentry and rehabilitating instead of just punishment. Gadsden was not like the state run prisons. You would be lucky to ever see the warden at a state run facility much less talk to one. But warden Molina would walk around the compound talking to the girls even eating the same food as we did in the chow hall. I was very impressed with his concept and he showed us all respect something we weren't used to in prison. He inspired the girls to better themselves and to get an education. Gadsden offered more educational programs, vocational, and betterment classes than any of the other Florida prisons put together.

I had become very close with quite a few women there at Gadsden and met some awesome people inside the walls. I was nearing the end of my sentence and on May 1, 2012 I signed to go to work release where I would live at a work release center and work on the outside. I knew it would be hard for me to leave Gadsden especially Donna my best friend and confident, Perez who would have made Cesar Milan proud, my little baby Virginia who made me laugh and started everyone calling me Grammy, GiGi who could get me fired up one minute and then we would be all about the dogs the next. I think I'm especially proud of GiGi for always taking constructive criticism and for coming so far since she started the dog program. There's so many Kelly, Ashley, Michelle who had been with me since the very beginning, Dixie, Heather, Michelle, CeeCee and Kristy, all who are still behind the walls. I know they say you come in alone you leave alone but if you're fortunate enough to touch other peoples' lives and your life is affected as well then you have done the right thing and they are not forgotten like so many other people have forgotten all those still locked up. Plus this was the place where I had made a profound change in my life. This was where I had come to a crossroad and started to see my vision of a different life one filled with meaning and purpose.

I think families are the worst sometimes and when you are in prison you are forgotten until you get out and even then many aren't supportive and many have returned to prison because they had no support system when they got out. After serving time in prison a person changes sometimes for the better but sometimes for the worse. So a lot of times someone gets out of prison and their family no longer knows that person. There is a transition getting used to being back in society. I refused to forget and vowed to someday return to the prison systems to continue to help educate our youth today. So my journey continued and I continued to grow. On September 13, 2012, I left Gadsden to go to the Suncoast work release center in St. Petersburg, Florida. It was a very emotional time for me. I had been at Gadsden for 6 years. My best friend Donna wrote me a poem that brought tears to my eyes and every time that I would doubt myself I would pull out that poem and read it. She also saw that I had a dream and she believed in me. She wanted me to go out and live out my dream and most of all she knew I could do it. I had never had anyone believe in me like that besides my mother.

While I was preparing to leave I pulled out the newsletter that Rob and Lucinda Boyd had sent me. In it was their mission statement which I had read but I don't think it had actually sunk in till now. This is what they were trying to tell me and everyone else out there in the movement. This was their key to success and everyone that followed it. It says....

TSDLYB MISSION STATEMENT

It is our mission to be a force for positive change and inspire others to greatness.

We will trust our dreams and be the prisoner of nothing.

We will strive to continually invent the future out of our imagination rather than be victims of the past.

We will live to the principles of charity, honesty, integrity, courage, justice, humility, kindness, respect, loyalty to self, trust, knowledge, understanding and non-violence.

We will use our personal defeats and victories unselfishly to help enrich the lives of all who cross our path by caring and affirming their unique worth, by giving what we have to give and teaching them what we know.

We will strive to educate others about the dangers of gang violence and drug activity and that there are many alternatives to the "gang/thug/drug" life.

We will encourage others to rise up and believe that they can achieve whatever they want in life.

We will embrace and see each day as not just another day, but one filled with opportunity and excitement as we remember that the pursuit of happiness and excellence will determine the choices we make and the paths we choose to travel.

We choose to make a difference in this world.

This is what they were trying to tell me when I was still inside prison. My dreams can come true and I can help make other people's dreams come true as well.

It was very hard for me to say goodbye to my last dog Atreyu. I had named him after the Indian boy in the Neverending story that rode Falcor on his quest. Now I would begin my quest and search out my dream. It had been 12 years since I had been on the outside. So much had changed little simple things like even using a cell phone was new to me. I felt my confidence level dropping again because it was a whole new world out here. My case worker Ms. Cullen was so patient and would always tell me to take a deep breath. She would work with me and give me guidance as I started to adjust to re-entry into society. I knew I could always come to her if I had any problems or just needed to talk. There were times she would just share a song on her cell phone with me and she always posted positive sayings on her blackboard in her office. She was a mother to so many girls there and a positive force. Ms. Dunmore the director who everyone dreaded being called in her office was one of the most passionate and caring woman for her girls that I have ever met. At first I was a little intimidated by her because she has such a powerful personality. But I soon learned she was just dedicated to helping the women there. For Halloween she hired a DJ and we had a costume party. She paid for everything out of her pocket, drinks, coffee, snacks, personnel pan pizzas and bags of Halloween candy. To me this was such a wonderful contrast to the life I had been living in prison. It showed me people do care for felons. Ms. Sherman the assistant director was one of the most patient and encouraging woman who I knew I could always turn to if I just needed to talk. Right away I felt very comfortable with her. She had one of the sweetest personalities. The rest of the staff was just as caring Ms. Saydeh, Ms. Aldridge, Mr. McSwain, Mr. Wagner, Mr. Marks, Mr. D. and so many others as well. It was a wonderful program and I was grateful I had worked so hard to get there. My first two weeks I had chest pains every time I went out to look for a job. I was so anxious after being locked up so many years and here I found myself back out and it was a whole new world out there. When you're out you don't see all the changes because they're slow but for someone like me it was a completely different place. I would come back in and talk to Ms. Cullen and she would always be so calm and positive breath Donna. I was very quiet in the beginning not saying much. I continued to search for jobs calling them back letting them know I was very interested. All the effort paid off and I got my first job at Subway. My boss was Doreen Richard and she knew my background and told me she believed everyone deserved a second chance. She was awesome and very patient with me.

Working a normal job was not something I was used to but I enjoyed it. I was only working part time there so when I was off I would continue to search for another job. I remember I met this girl at a bus stop and she asked if I was work release. People used to be able to pick us out probably because most of us looked lost in the beginning. I told her I was and that I was looking for a second job. She gave me a business card and told me to call Bill Rush Monday morning or just come in and see him at the Holiday Inn. That's where she worked and they were looking for another waitress. I decided to go in person so on my day off that Tuesday I went in there and had an interview with Bill Rush. He explained the position and hired me right on the spot. I still remember how I felt when I walked out of there. I felt like jumping up in the air. I had waited so many years to just get to work release and to be given a second chance and I was finding out there are plenty of people willing to give you that second chance if you just showed you wanted to change. I was very nervous working at a new place and I made plenty of mistakes but the head waitress Tanya was very helpful and Bill was wonderful and supportive. My coworker Greg O was always giving me encouraging words and showing me the latest Lee Child book. I used to get up at 4:00 A.M. and leave at 5:00 A.M. to be at work at 6:00 A.M., work till 11:30 A.M. then go to Subway and work till 3:00 P.M.

I was trying to save money for when I got out so I decided to get one more job. There was a McDonalds across the street from Subway and the Holiday Inn so I filled out an application and was thrilled to be hired there as well from 3:00 P.M. to 11:00 P.M.

Now I had three jobs and my confidence level on the outside was building. I liked working and staying active. I would take as many hours as I could get. There was a class on Wednesday nights called Infinite Possibilities that I tried not to ever miss. There were two ladies that volunteered and taught the class. It was all about positive thinking and positive attitudes. I loved it because I believe if you surround yourself with negative people you're going to have negative results but if you surround yourself with positive people and positive attitudes than you will have positive results in your life. I always like to think good about things and most of the time I'm in a positive frame of mind. It meant a lot to the girls in there that Mimi and Elizabeth came in on their own time to spend time with us. They are truly remarkable women. I continued to work out at

Suncoast whenever I wasn't working. I had a workout partner who I knew from Gadsden. Her name was Welkner and I was very proud at how far she had come in her life.

There are some people that you know are going to succeed and she was one of them. She had worked so hard to change her life around taking betterment classes and substance abuse classes. There were so many girls that I had met while I was in prison and they all had a part in changing me to who I am today. Working with them is what made me want to help and educate the youth today.

Everything was going well at work release until around the end of December a guy from the Goodwill men's work release was accused of killing two men and setting their house on fire. That brought a lot of bad press to the entire work release center. Not even a month later another man was accused of raping and beating a young girl from the same work release center. The community was upset that violent offenders were being housed at work release. Unfortunately a representative from Goodwill had made a comment that there were no violent offender's housed there and the St. Petersburg paper investigated and found that there were hundreds of violent offenders throughout the state.

On the morning of March 1, 2013 I was woken up at 4:45 A.M. and told I was going back to prison. They told me I had done nothing wrong but I was going back. I knew right away that it was because of what had happened at the men's work release program and they were sending all violent offenders back. So many emotions went through me, most of all I was hurt. Here I had tried so hard to change my life and I felt that all the accomplishments I had achieved didn't matter. There were three of us from Suncoast work release center that were sent back. One of the girls only had 10 days left before her release.

They took us to Hernando Correctional Institution where we were processed then placed into general population. The warden met us and said once again we had done nothing wrong that it was just a policy change. It was all politics. I felt like I was being punished for something I hadn't done. There were a lot of emotions anger, hurt, and shock to be back in prison. After the shock wore off I told myself I refused to let this stop me and I would find out what Gods plan was for me. I knew there was a reason why I had to go through another tribulation. So I started looking around to see what the prison offered as far as wellness and education. Because I only had four months left to do I couldn't take any classes. They only had one vocational class called Desktop. They did have an excellent GED program that was having a lot of success. There were hardly any wellness classes so I wrote the recreation supervisor with a proposition for a wellness class. He wrote me back denying it. So I decided I would start working out and encouraging the other girls to join me. It did not take long before there was quite a group of us working out doing circuit training classes on our own. It was inspiring to me to see girls who never worked out getting involved. They wanted something to connect with, something positive to get involved in and it wasn't long before other girls were starting their own workout classes. I remember one day just sitting back watching everybody interact. I was so proud of all of them and I thought to myself these girls are so much a part of my life. I vowed it wouldn't stop here that I would one day come back inside to share my story. I did some tutoring in the dorm and started to talk to the young girls about what they planned to do when they got out. Sharing the resources I had for halfway houses or financial help.

I figured my work wasn't done in prison and God brought me back so I would never forget and show me the beginning of the plan he had for my life. I remained positive even though it was hard at times. The months started to go by and I was becoming close to a lot of the girls. One lady that had recently just come to prison used to call me her voice of reason because I was always keeping it real with her and giving her advice. I wrote Beverly Sebastian with the National Greyhound Foundation and told her I was back in prison and that I would be released July 4, 2013 and expressed my desire to work for her upon my release.

I had so many things I wanted to do when I got out so many dreams. I wanted to work with the youth against drugs and violence and domestic violence and the greyhound foundation. I had spent years dreaming about this and my time was almost done. It was a very exciting time. I was still writing Rob and Lucinda Boyd and receiving news letters from them. At the time I had no idea that when I got released I would join their movement TSDLYB and start to live out my dream.

The girl who slept next to me had an MP3 player and she told me to listen to a song on it. She said she had heard me talk of my mother so much that it made her think of me. I would listen to that song every day until I left. It was Ozzy Osborne," Mama I'm coming home." How appropriate after 13 years to hear a song knowing I was on my way home to my Mother. Nothing could steal my joy before I left. Prison was always so loud and there is never any time for privacy and I always felt like I couldn't breathe. I think that's why I liked to work out so much, it gave me a little privacy when I would put my headphones on and work out. Nobody could take that away from me. It was my time to get away.

Everybody has their own way of dealing with prison. Some get into religion, working out, or doing the education thing. But of course the majority is still into the street scene but it's inside the walls. I'll never forget my last night at Hernando.

When someone is released the inmates always give a Home Cadence saying goodbye. Well it was the last count of the evening and I only had a few hours left before I got out. One of the girls that I had been encouraging and working out with stood up and said Donna Buchanan has been down for 13 years and she's going home tonight. Everyone started clapping their hands and stomping on lockers. They were all just clapping and I looked around at all 71 girls one by one and what I saw on their faces told me I had made an impact on their lives and this was what I was meant to do.

These girls... from the streets... that don't love you back, were a part of my past and future. I vowed to never forget the ones left inside and the ones yet to come. This is what God brought me back to prison, to show me what I was meant to do with my life. This was God's plan, to educate the youth today.

I was released and flew to Richmond to stay with my family. My first day out I spoke to Rob and Lucinda Boyd and was able to thank them for all their support. They sent me a box of t-shirts and a lot of info on jobs for ex-offenders and resources. I spoke to Mr. Boyd and he encouraged me to tell my story. Within a week I had a face book page and within two weeks I had a website called Second Chance Runaway named after my book. I named it Second Chance Runaway for three reasons: One because I had started out my life running away and two I was given a second chance at life and three for the Second Chance at Life dog program which helped change my life and healed my life as I worked with the dogs. It just seemed so perfect.

Rob and Lucinda became my managers and booked me for a radio show interview on their radio show August 7, 2013. I continued to be in contact with them and soon I was writing my book. Before long I had several radio shows booked.

July 24, 2013 I was on the DJ Church show

July 24, 2013 I was on with Katherine

August 5, 2013 I was on Talk to CoGee

August 7, 2013 I was on the Boyd & Lucinda Show

August 11, 2013 I was on the Cypher Den Show

August 16, 2013 I was on Freedom Door Ministries.

All these interviews within a couple of weeks was amazing.

July 25, 2013 the Buckeye Valley News an Arizona newspaper did an article on me welcoming me home. I just couldn't believe how much God was blessing my life. My dreams were becoming a reality. Lucinda Boyd agreed to edit my book so I began to tell my story and start to educate the youth today. I cannot change my past and I'm not ashamed of my past. It is what it is. But what matters is what I do with my future and the futures of others.

On July 30, 2013 Beverly Sebastian called me and said she had two dogs that she needed trained for service for a veteran. I began to work with her and once again another part of my dream was coming true.

On August 1, 2013 Beverly and Ferd posted the veteran and dog on her website. The veteran that I'm going to train the dog for is Rey Martinez and the greyhounds name is Roo. I had thought of working with her and the greyhound foundation for years in prison now was my chance was becoming a reality.

If someone tells you your dreams can't come true I would like to remind you they do come true. Look at me I'm spreading the message to the youth today and training dogs. My mom always believed in me and never gave up on me unconditionally loving me. Without her I would have been lost to the darkness while everyone counted me out. I am not to be counted out and I will tell my story to make a change in other people's lives.

Now I had the support of Rob and Lucinda Boyd and Beverly and Ferd Sebastian. I now have a purpose in life to tell my story. My goal is to tell everyone, The Streets Don't Love You Back. I am a success story!

DONNA BUCHANAN

SECOND CHANCE RUNAWAY

DONNA'S PICTURES

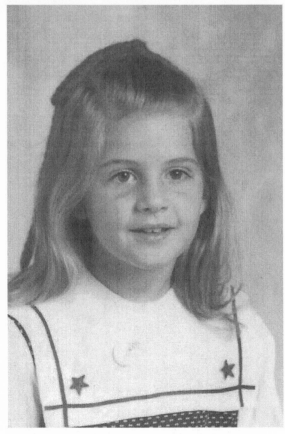

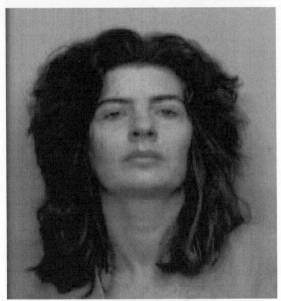

DONNA'S MUGSHOT

Commencement Program

Gadsden Correctional Facility

November 6, 2009

Processional .... Graduates

Welcome .... Ms. Rhonda Craig

Master of Ceremony .... Mr. Brewster Banks

Project H.E.R. .... Music Selection

Introduction of Speaker .... Ms. Rhonda Craig

Speaker .... Sherrie Taylor
Gadsden County Commissioner

Praise Dance .... Praise Dance Team

Intro of Valedictorian & Salutatorian .... Mr. Eric Byrd

Valedictorian .... Jamie Smith

Salutatorian .... Renata Brown

Certificate Presentation .... Mr. Byrd, GED
Ms. Johnson, Law Clerk
Ms. Knorp, Auto Cad
Mr. Banks, Building Constructions
Ms. Lewis, Cosmetology
Chef Ross, Culinary Art
Ms. Craig, CDL
Mr. Swan, Horticulture
Ms. D'Entremont, PC Support

Band .... Music Selection

Original Poetry Reading "Knowledge" .... Dady Mercy

Closing Remarks .... Ms. Rhonda Craig

Luncheon Immediately Following for Guests and Graduates

GED

Jamie Smith, Valedictorian
Renata Brown, Salutatorian
Janet Amundson
Jessica Cybah
Tracy Franklin
Alicia Griffin
Roselynn McCullough

Law Clerk

Angela McDonald
Carolyn Stewart

AutoCAD

Donna Buchanan
Sava Buchanan
Tammy Burchfield
Angela Clemmons
Jacqueline Reynolds
Andrea Williams

Building Construction

Alison Brown
Donna Duffee
Gacela Solomon

Cosmetology

Kulsha Lewis

Culinary Arts

Suzanne Bainbridge
Christina Cooper
Jennifer Curran

CDL

Mindy Bigay
Winifred Carter
Frahasia Davis
Valerie Delaney
Audrey Dodd
Angela Fuesta
Nicolle Gewett
Rebecca Gray
Dianeshia Johnson
Corri Johnston
Cassandra Lee
Leanne Lee
Lakesha Lewis
Dady Mercy
Kaycy Mitchell
Ayana Moose
Nakia Oliver
Sabrina Padgette
Linda Perry
Chanta Roebuck
Toni Sawyer
Joanna Seaman
Cynthia Thomson
Amy Warren
Eva Marie White

Horticulture

Dana Cooper
Lisa Cuestavasa
Lisa Pritchett
Wendy Shepard
Bridget Sunbury

PC Support

Lisa Batchelder
Joni Davis
Samantha Skipper

DONNA'S GRADUATION
Gadsden Correctional Facility
November 6, 2009

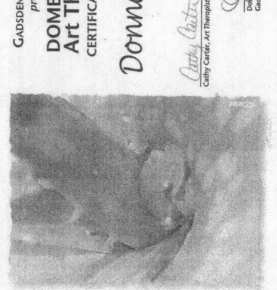

GADSDEN CORRECTIONAL FACILITY
proudly presents this

**DOMESTIC VIOLENCE
Art Therapy Group**
CERTIFICATE OF PARTICIPATION
to

Donna Buchanan

Cathy Carter, Art Therapist

Nicole Wade, Art Therapist

Donna Kitch, PhD, Psychologist
Gadsden Correctional Facility

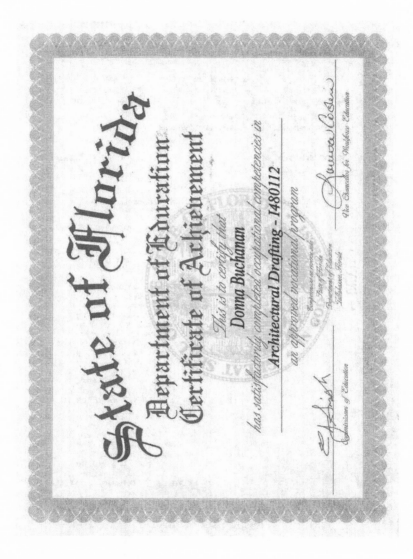

Certificate of Completion

For

Intro to Vet Tech Program

This certificate is awarded to

DONNA BUCHANAN

Completion for a 32 Hour Intro to Vet Tech Program

Signature Robin Conrad, Canine Program Coordinator

12/31/2009

Date

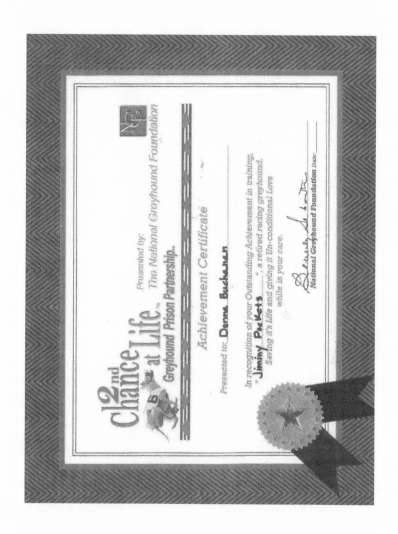

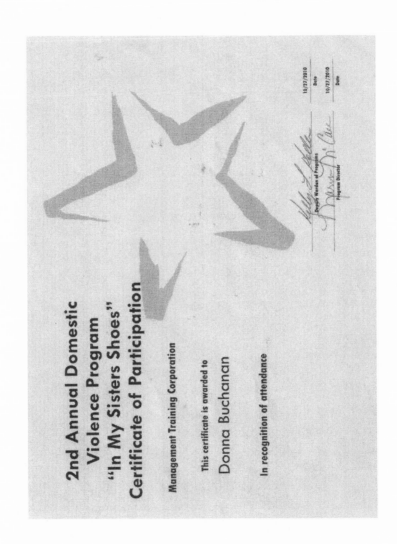

2nd Annual Domestic
Violence Program
"In My Sisters Shoes"
Certificate of Participation

Management Training Corporation

This certificate is awarded to

Donna Buchanan

In recognition of attendance

Deputy Warden of Programs   10/27/2010
                                                Date

Program Director   10/27/2010
                                                Date

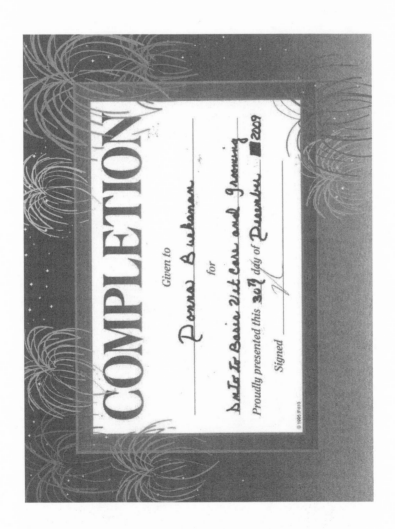

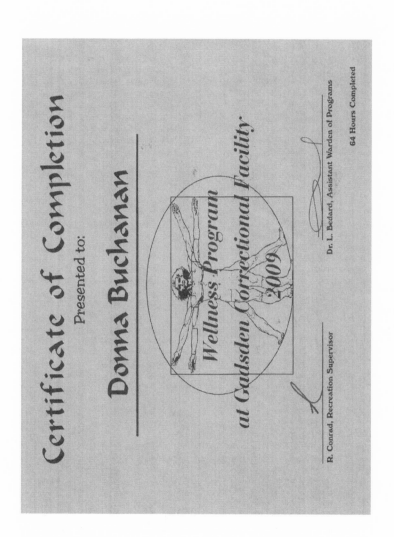

Certificate of Completion

Presented to:

Donna Buchanan

Wellness Program
at Gadsden Correctional Facility
2009

R. Conrad, Recreation Supervisor

Dr. L. Bedard, Assistant Warden of Programs

64 Hours Completed

Infinite Possibilities

Certificate of Completion

Earned and Awarded to

Donna Buchanan

We hope that we have
Inspired Balance, Instilled a Heart Sense
And
Enlightened you to your Infinite Possibilities.
Remember
Thoughts Become Things . . . .Choose The Good Ones!

Mimi & Elizabeth

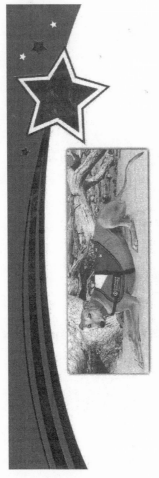

THIS CERTIFIES THAT, JNS FLOPO GUYPO, "FALCOR", HAS COMPLETED ALL REQUIRED TESTS AND IS NOW A, "PURPLE HEART GREYHOUND SERVICE DOG."

Thanks to his Trainers:___Donna Buchanan___

Beverly Sebastian _Beverly Sebastian_ date 6/7/12
CEO National Greyhound Foundation

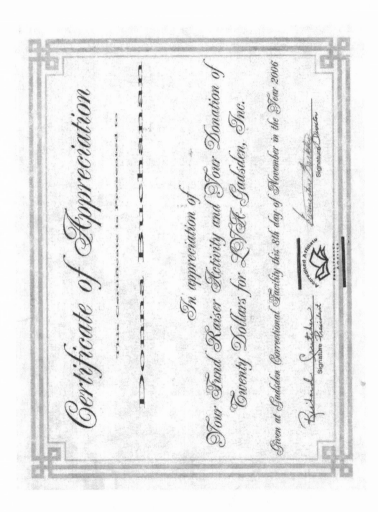

Donna was the trainer of this service dog named JNS Guypo (falcor) while at Gadsen Correctional Facility

Inmate Donna Buchanan, left, who trained Falcor for four months, instructs Leisel Luman and daughter, Abby, in the handling of their new dog at Gadsden Correctional Facility. Luman is a U.S. Army veteran diagnosed with PSTD and needs the dog to cope with crowds and public places. (July 18, 2012) (Herald-Tribune staff photos by Dan Wagner)

SECOND CHANCE RUNAWAY

A LETTER FROM DONNA'S FRIEND

Been a long time coming -it's here at last
You're leaving this place and leaving the past
The memories we share cannot be lost
The price of friendship - There is no cost.

Three years ago, you cooked us a meal
a short time later, our friendship was real
we've talked and talked, and laughed and cried
We spoke truth to each other, we never lied.

Our first dogs, we trained them together
You took off running, getting better and better
You made a name for yourself in this doggy place
The dogs you trained did an about face.

You may not be blood, but you're close to my heart
I knew this day would come, we'd be apart
you do your best, in all you do
And this you'll continue in a world that's new

Its going to be tough, being left right here
You'll be long gone, no longer near.
But, I tell you, my friend, I'm so very glad
As your the best friend I've ever had.

A new life for you - its about to start
The minutes - each ticking - like the beats of a heart
You learned all you could on this dog team
Take it to your dog world - and live out your dream.

Donna,
   This was the most difficult poems
I've written. You mean a lot to me
and have been so much a part of my
life in here. Thanks for always being
there even when I didn't want you
to be. You somehow always know.
To say I'm going to miss you is an
understatement. You will always
be in my thoughts and prayers.
So Get Em!!
              Love
              Donna

DONNA AND HER MOTHER, LINDA

THANK YOU

MOM

FOR ALWAYS BEING THERE FOR ME!

Robert and Lucinda Boyd

The Streets Don't Love You Back Movement

www.thestreetsdontloveyouback.com

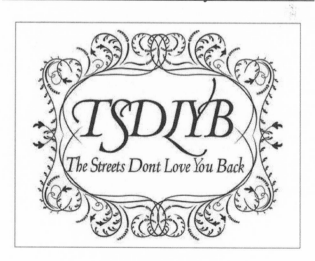

SECOND CHANCE RUNAWAY

Mission Statement

It is our mission to be a force for positive change and inspire others to greatness.

We will trust our dreams and be the prisoner of nothing.

We will strive to continually invent the future out of our imagination rather than be victims of the past.

We will live true to the principles of charity, honesty, integrity, courage, justice, humility, kindness, respect, loyalty to self, trust, knowledge, understanding and non-violence.

We will use our personal defeats and victories unselfishly to help enrich the lives of all who cross our path by caring and affirming their unique worth, by giving what we have to give and teaching them what we know.

We will strive to educate others about the dangers of gang violence and drug activity and that there are many alternatives to the "gang/thug/drug" life.

We will encourage others to rise up and believe that they can be a greater person and believe that they can achieve whatever they want in life.

We will embrace and see each day as not just another day, but one filled with opportunity and excitement as we remember that the pursuit of happiness and excellence will determine the choices we make and the paths we choose to travel.

We choose to make a difference in this world.

SECOND CHANCE RUNAWAY

Made in the USA
San Bernardino, CA
14 December 2014